Paula
much love
Dec. 2016
Mum & dad

a way home

For Sam

a way home

Building a new life and a strawbale house
in Central Otago — one woman's inspirational story

JILLIAN SULLIVAN

pb potton & burton

Contents

Author's Note

I am aware new laws for today's building sites promote health and safety, with workers protected by safety nets and fenced scaffolding. The journey I took with Sam was physical, and metaphorical. When he told me to 'walk that beam like there's no tomorrow,' he was teaching me to act with purpose and courage. And when we live this way, there is – as Sam also taught me – 'no such thing as can't.'

Prologue

In my previous life, living on a small block of land near Tasman Bay, I came home from town one day with some poems written on postcards. It was New Zealand Book Month. The poems were from books shortlisted for the national book award for poetry. I wrote a few postcards and mailed them, but one I particularly liked I propped against the vase of flowers on my table, and there it stayed for weeks. It was a poem called 'What It's Like', by Brian Turner. He lived in the small village of Oturehua, in Central Otago, though I didn't know that when I brought the poem home, nor did I know much about the poet, except at one stage he'd been New Zealand Poet Laureate. This is what it said:

> When someone asks you to explain
> what it's like where you come from
> you say you're still finding out,
> and it's not because you enjoy being
> vague, or smart-arse, a sophist
> if you like, it's just because it's true.
>
> This morning frost then fog-like smoke
> from a damp wood fire, then the sun
> breaking through in lamé-like patches
> until there's not even bandannas
> left on the hills, and order's restored:
> blue sky above incandescent snow.

In my new life, I'd bought a piece of land down south, in the Ida Valley. I would one day live myself where wood smoke plumed above a frosted roof. That poem had leant against the vase of changing flowers on my table, breathing of the sky and mountain land where I would end up living two years in the future.

It was time to pack up my belongings and put them in storage. I had to sort through every drawer and every box of papers, for I didn't know how long it would be till I had a home again, and what I would need, what I could store and what I could safely throw away.

Every letter was read; every photo looked at while I sat on the couch. It was sunny, early summer. I played Chris Knox, Bob Dylan, Cymande, Leonard Cohen while I sorted. Photos of babies and a growing family; photos of Marie the goat I milked by hand for years for the children; the dogs we had, my wedding day photo, with my grandparents, now dead, and my dad, now dead, and my first husband now married to someone else. Memories of lost love surged and almost overwhelmed me. The time when I was busy with five children seemed another life to where I was now, undone and let go.

In the middle of a box of papers, amongst fragments of poems and short stories and old bank statements, I came across a sealed envelope dated 1998, addressed to myself in the future, something I'd done as an exercise out of a book once and then forgotten about.

I opened the envelope and read the page inside. It said:

I live in a strawbale house, looking out to the mountains.

WOOD

*It may be that when we no longer know what to do,
we have come to our real work
and when we no longer know which way to go,
we have begun our real journey.*

– WENDELL BERRY, *STANDING BY WORDS*, 1983

CHAPTER 1

A Starting Place

The day we packed up our vehicles with the first load of building materials and tools, it was mid-November, the sky a wide blue vault above us. My son-in-law Sam Deavoll had left his building job and taken on the task of helping me build my strawbale house. We had a summer to get the frame up, ready for the straw. I had no idea of what was ahead of us.

I was unfit, unskilled and fifty-five years old.

We drove through the tawny, rocky Central Otago landscape, past the towns of Cromwell and Alexandra, where we stopped for food and supplies, up over Tiger Hill, through Omakau and at last into the Ida Valley, the blue pleats of the Hawkdun mountain range rising ahead of us.

At the far end of the village of Oturehua, we went through an old gate, over long grass and onto the building site.

'Do you want to be treated like a grandmother or like a builder?' Sam asked me.

'I want to be treated like a builder.'

'Good,' he said, 'because that way you'll do far more than you think is possible.'

My old life had ended (children left home, marriage over), though my life as a writer continued. And now a builder, for I had the chance to help build my own home. And because I would live in the coldest valley in the country, and I wanted a natural home, one that inexperienced people could work on, I'd chosen to build with straw.

If ever there are distinct chapters to your life, then I knew this day marked the beginning of an important chapter in mine. There'd been a lot to get through to reach this moment: the grief of partings, the unknown and searching, the risk and joys of finding and buying the land and making new alliances. There was the phase of getting permits and easements, not to forget the planning, the designs, the engineering, the consents.

And now here Sam and I were. We parked by the newly planted temporary power box, beside the scraped building site, a square that encompassed the future building of a cottage, 10 metres by 10.7.

Sam jumped out and started pulling off the long 8×2s that were to be our boxing timber, and later on the scaffolding, though I couldn't imagine that yet. For now I had fresh peeled earth and green fields around it.

A blank page on which to begin a new life.

Carl Jung, who built himself a stone house following the death of his mother, talked about the parallels of building a dwelling and reconstructing a life. After loss, he assembled himself again with his tower at Bollingen, 'a representation in stone of my innermost thoughts...'

I thought of this when Sam passed me the spade and grubber. We were going to dig the foundations by hand. If loss means a life taken back to bedrock, then I was here at bedrock; nothing between me and the soil but my feet in boots braced on the earth and only sky above me.

First we set up the string lines and demarked the line of the walls. Then I hefted the grubber in my hands. Over and over I dropped it into the ground, breaking up the clods, opening up a seam in the soil. Sam worked ahead of me, banging in the pegs with a sledgehammer and screwing on the foundation boxing. I scooped out earth with a spade, and the ditch grew smoother, the space for safe foundations grew deeper.

Instead of digging the trench to the desired depth in one go, a daunting task in that hard packed earth, Sam had us dig once around the perimeter of the building to start the channel, then around again, deepening it, then again and again, each circuit hollowing out the ditch closer to the required depth of 500 millimetres.

Jung, when digging his foundations, found a whole skeleton, a photo of which is kept in his stone tower. I hoped I didn't find any skeletons.

Sam finished putting the boxing up and took over the grubber from me. He went ahead breaking the soil in a long channel, and I only had to follow and clear it, one spadeful at a time, favouring my blistered right hand and then my left.

By lunch time the next day I was so sore and tired I didn't know what to do with my body. I couldn't dig or eat. I climbed the wire fence between my place and my new neighbour, the poet Brian Turner, and went up to his house for a cup of tea and some succour.

'I can hardly move,' I told him. So he read me a poem of Auden's, and we sat in the old chairs on his porch, looking out to the schist stone wall and the birds hopping amongst the branches of the crabapple tree.

'I'll come and do some digging with you once I've hoed the potatoes,' Brian said. He turned up on site later with his own grubber and spade, heavy gloves on his hands, but we were miraculously finished. The ditch we began yesterday and seemed would go on forever, around and around the perimeter, was completed. We stood back and looked at the shape of the house Sam and I would build together.

'That's the hardest physical work done,' said Sam. 'It will be easier after this.' I believed him then, and thought I *had* done the hardest part and all would be simple from then on.

To celebrate the footings, Sam climbed onto the cable drum and leapt from it with grubber and spade flying so I could get a photo. His acrobatic zaniness a pleasing foil to the way I felt inside, as if every organ had been displaced and moved around and wasn't quite back where it should be.

Brian put his grubber and spade down, probably with relief, and we celebrated with beers instead, the three of us in the sun.

When my second marriage ended in 2010, my friend Joy Cowley had said to me, 'If a door shuts that fast and soundly in your life, it means another door is already open.' And she passed on some advice that an older woman had given her: 'Don't ever let yourself be bitter.' With that, I had determined to look upon the time of loss as an opportunity for a new way of living. I didn't want to dwell on the fact that I had to leave my home and garden and my horse Rosie and make my way in a world, not knowing where to go or how I would live or even who I wanted to be. A door already open? I couldn't see that, and turned and turned looking.

Later I understood the door was open onto a new vista, that of the golden, tussocked hills, craggy tors and folded mountains of Central Otago, the high desert plateau in the deep south of New Zealand. I only had to find my way to that door and go through it.

Having five grown-up children spread out round the country and overseas meant I had a range of places to choose where to live to be near family. But which way to go? I thought I would go back near my hometown of Masterton, close to the city of Wellington where I was completing a Master's degree. I studied properties on Trade Me and in real estate pages. I looked at cheap hillside sections in the city, at houses or rural sections outside of small towns in the North Island. But nothing made sense. In the end I would somehow have to make a life and get my joy back, my understanding of who I was.

One day on a road trip down south to visit my daughter Hana and Sam and grandchildren in Queenstown, I stopped off in the Mackenzie Country. I walked

Sam celebrates the completed trench and boxing.

down to the Twizel River and stood watching the light. The water moved clearly and cleanly over the stones and boulders. Upriver between a framework of willows were mountains: snow-covered Aoraki and the Southern Alps. There on those grey river stones I remembered what I loved: rocks and stones and light on water and the shapes of mountains in the sun.

This was when I knew I had a starting place. There were perhaps more sensible choices: to be nearer extended family in the North Island, to be nearer a town or city. But a river was my starting point. I would stay in the South Island. I would live where I could see the mountains and the hills. And with that image I began my search for land.

I would buy somewhere within an hour and a half of my daughter and grandchildren. I would buy a place near water. I wanted running water of some kind, for I had once lived for 17 years beside the sea. The tides and the light on the water and the seabirds and the sky had been a solace and bringer of joy. And I would buy a place as inexpensive as possible, so I could afford to live as a writer.

The pond on my land in the coldest place in New Zealand.

I set out on a five-day journey in my car and drove around the lower half of the South Island, through the hills and desert plains of Central Otago. There I found a rough piece of land, twenty acres, unkempt, ungrazed, with a multitude of access problems and bogginess I was yet to discover. It was cheap, and it was in the coldest (a record -25°C) and hottest (over 40°C) district in New Zealand. Best of all, though, it had running water along its boundary; the Ida Burn stream.

I'd wanted to build a house of natural materials since first reading about them in Alister Taylor's *New Zealand Whole Earth Catalogue*. As a teenager, I had read books on stone houses, on mud-brick houses, on rammed-earth houses, and a book on all the weird and inspiring and creative dwellings that people had crafted for themselves. When I read about strawbale houses, years ago, I could see they would have the thick-walled beauty of mud-brick or stone, but with the lightness of construction and the sustainability of straw. I decided then I wanted to have a strawbale home one day, and to build it myself with friends and family and those who just turned up to help. I loved the idea that anyone could build a house.

Standing there on the rough piece of land for sale, named Bastard Flats, it occurred to me that I could finally have the chance to help build my own home. I took photos of the Ida Burn stream, and back at my daughter's house in Queenstown I considered the photos again, wondering if I would be able to shift to an isolated valley and take care of that piece of land. A small valley of such extremes. I looked across to the fridge, and written in chalk on a black poster, Hana had copied this quote, often attributed to Goethe:

Whatever you can do or dream you can, begin it.
Boldness has genius, power and magic in it.

Filled with the timely strength of the words, and before I could change my mind or anyone came home and asked me sensible questions, I picked up the phone and rang the real estate agent. When Hana and Sam came home, I told them I'd bought the piece of land in Central Otago, and how the quote on the fridge had helped me. Hana walked over and rubbed the quote off straight away. She said, 'That's so you don't go and do anything else risky.'

CHAPTER 2

Foundations

My grandfather owned a factory for making plaster sheets for houses. My father, George, and Uncle Ken, identical twins, had to leave school at age 16 and work in the family business. That first day of work, my father said, was the longest day of his life. The twins stayed plasterers for the next 55 years, and if they had longed for other lives – to be orchardists, to be cricketers – they subdued these ideas and became respected craftsmen.

The factory was a dimly lit corrugated iron building with large benches the size and shape of plaster sheets. It was so cold in winter the men crouched over a coal fire that burned in an old kerosene tin. They warmed their hands at smoko, sitting round the glowing coals, wearing plaster-spattered white overalls, with nail boxes for their seats and their lunches in tin pails beside them.

Rats ran along the rafters, and whistling spiders lived in the sacks of plaster. Or so the twins were told, and for months they knocked the sides of each sack before opening it to make sure the mythical spiders had run away.

I was sometimes taken down to the factory on a Saturday morning. I watched my father pour the plaster mix across the face of the greased bench. He filled the fluid plaster with handfuls of toe, South African hemp, that he'd teased out from a large compressed bale. The toe put fibre and strength into the sheets. I was allowed to press the toe in too. The plaster mix was cool and silky on my fingers. I pushed in the curly strands of hemp, like long pieces of sawdust, until they were submerged.

Once hardened, the sheets were lifted and carried outside to dry in the sheds. In winter, the twins lit kerosene fires beneath the sheets to dry them.

This was how houses were built in Masterton up to the 1970s: with walls that were mixed and pressed by hands, even a child's, and from materials whose origin we knew: plaster from powdered rock, toe from dried hemp stalks. The benches were greased with mutton fat.

The texture of mud needed for plastering my strawbale house, six months into the project, was not that different from my father's plaster mix. I made the mud mix for my house in a concrete mixer and watched as the drum flipped over and over, tumbling the sand and clay and water. I fed in handfuls of teased-out straw to bind the silky mud, much as my father had pushed in toe, both of us constructing walls out of materials from the land.

Children growing up now are digital natives, born into the technology of computers and social media. I grew up in the typewriter era. I began my paid writing life at age 17 as cub reporter on the *Hawera Star*, with my very own Imperial 66 typewriter, bought at great cost and trepidation for $75. Each of us in the newsroom at the *Hawera Star* had our own desk and our own typewriter, and during the 1975 election, our own political party to cover (I had Labour). We competed for coverage of speeches and political rallies, although the editor, a whisky-drinking Scotsman, made our column inches tally with each other. Everything fair in journalism, then.

In the 1990s, when I purchased my first computer, a second-hand Commodore 64, I could barely control it. I lost quarter of a novel; I lost for a time a manuscript into the hard drive. Some days I lay my head on my arms and wept in frustration. Now my pre-school grandchildren move their way confidently around an iPad. I still know only the bare necessities to get by on my laptop. I was born into a world centred on a concrete mixer and a trowel.

My father apprenticed all three of my brothers into the plastering firm, George Masters & Sons Ltd. My sisters and I weren't taught the family trade. When I visited Dad on building sites and sat with him on a nail-box seat, sharing his chocolate biscuits and a cup of tea from his thermos, I wished I was a worker there, too, part of the team.

I think about the way in which we have been affected by the past and, in turn, what we pass on to our children. When I was six my mother took me into her bedroom and showed me stories hidden away in her drawer; stories she'd written for children. I grew up to become a children's writer, with concrete mixers and fluid building materials imprinted in my brain.

By the time my son Nick was three, we'd shifted to live beside the sea. He left home at age 18 on a yacht and crisscrossed the world as a sailor. How much does chance play in what we become and in what we yearn to do?

And in what way, I wonder, has building the strawbale house affected my grandchildren? Indy, aged four, with her small bucket of mud and her own patch of wall to plaster. There she is, her hands in some of that fluid material, side by side with her family, her mind taking it in: this is how you can build a house, one handful at a time.

Growing up in Masterton, there were two things I could rely on: the support of my grandparents, Arch and Myrtle Wellington, who lived a ten-minute bike ride away from our house in Harley Street, and whom I saw every day, and my animals: a Siamese cat, Tunku, that I loved from the age of six, and from nine, my pony Gypsy. She was, in some ways, a violent pony; much taken to kicking me, biting, bolting, rearing, bucking, and throwing me on tarseal roads – once on my head, or so I discovered when I came to on an empty country road, my hands still clutching the reins and Gypsy standing above as if to protect me. Long enough, that was, until she could chase me again, sometimes right across the paddock. Yet I loved her fiercely and unconditionally.

Where this intense love of horses came from, my family couldn't work out. No one in our extended family had owned a horse or even ridden one. When I was young I would follow girls riding horses down our road, hoping one of them would notice my longing and give me a turn. All I had was Dad's sawhorse, which I'd set up under the willow tree and ride, wearing Dad's Wairarapa cricket uniform of blazer and cap. I drew horses incessantly, had imaginary horses that accompanied me everywhere. To say that being given my own pony (wild and unsuitable as she was) made me happy seems the greatest of understatements. I tried explaining how I felt once to my piano teacher, Miss Stubbings, and she said that's how she felt when, as a sixty year old, she finally purchased her own house. I politely listened to her reminiscing, but I didn't think owning a house had a patch on the happiness of having your own pony.

My parents' marriage was also wild and unsuitable. My father was a sportsman and a tradesman, my mother a musician and a teacher. They met as she walked past his cricket practice, on her way to piano lessons. My father and Ken were tall, lean men, with curly black hair, dark eyes and olive skin; athletic and agile. They excelled at every sport they played: New Zealand champion gymnasts, Wairarapa top-seed tennis players, and the same for badminton, Wairarapa bowlers and batsmen during cricket season, and both at once for my father, high divers and strong swimmers. The twins grew up obsessed with cricket, immediately going out to bowl for each other after school in eternal games that lasted till dark each night. The newspaper once referred to them as the New Zealand Bedsers (twin cricketers who played for England).

As young men, they could walk around with Dad standing on top of Ken's shoulders.

'I'd pretend to trip,' Uncle Ken told me, 'and George would fall and land doing a forward roll then he'd spring up again.' I can remember Dad walking on his hands down the steps and along the path to get the mail, and back again.

Mum's body was as soft as Dad's was lean. From age six Jeannine learnt the piano from the same Miss Stubbings I went to 30 years later. Mum's parents lived in a working-man's cottage in Bentley Street, down near the railway lines. It was a cold, wooden house, there were four children to care for and not enough money for a car. My grandfather Arch biked to work, his pressed trousers held safe by bicycle clips. Somehow they sacrificed enough to have money for my mother's music lessons. By age 14 she'd achieved Grade 8, Royal Schools of Music, and her music teaching letters, ATCL.

In between were rewarding years for her parents, especially Arch, who loved classical music. Mum would play his favourite pieces for him: Chopin's Nocturne in E Flat, Mozart's Minuet in G, Beethoven's Sonata in C Minor. On a Sunday night the Denbys came over and sang round the piano: 'Jeannine', 'I Dream of Lilac Time', 'Lily of Laguna', 'That Saxophone Waltz', and Grandad's favourite, 'Open Road, Open Sky'. Mum didn't have to know the tune. Hum a few bars, and she could play anything. If Uncle Vic Butland was there, he'd play his violin. Mum's older brothers and sister had to go to bed, but she was allowed to stay up and keep playing for the adults, for as long as they wanted to sing.

I have a photo of my mum at age 18 sitting at the organ in a church, the high leadlight windows behind her. And I have a photo of my grandfather and the twins as young men, in armchairs by the fire, the radio on the shelf, the three of them listening to the cricket.

My father and mother helped build their first house, living in the garage for a year while they did so. They turned the paddock surrounding it into a garden and lawns. My father, the orchardist who never left plastering, grew nectarines, peaches, apples, apricots, plums, grapes, lemons, red and black currant bushes and raspberries. In the middle of the trees was a vegetable garden, and a lawn where we played cricket.

I was the only child of the four of us who was taken out for piano lessons. Not as talented as my mother, yet in love with the music, Beethoven's Rondo in C my favourite. I made it to Grade 6 when I was 15, though always under threat from my mother she would sell Gypsy if I failed a music exam.

But there were no singing parties round the piano in our house, no 'Play Chopin for me, Jeannine.' Playing the piano wasn't encouraged until the housework was done, and it was never done with, my mother said. Four children in five years, and a life of housewifery in the 1960s, where how things looked was more important than how things really were, didn't suit my mother.

I asked her what was the hardest thing about being a housewife in those days? She said the ironing. 'It would build up and up. I couldn't get on top of it. It was always there.' Everything had to be ironed, the pillow cases, the tea towels, all the clothes. It was my job to iron the handkerchiefs.

In her unhappiness my mother put on more and more weight. She cried in shop dressing rooms when she tried to buy clothes that fitted. In one big push to lose weight, she taped photos of herself on every food cupboard in the kitchen. In her secret moments she wrote stories and songs.

My father played badminton in the evenings, mixed doubles with partners who shared his joy in the game. Silences opened up between my parents, and an escalation of violent arguments.

The marriage came to a crisis the day Mum found out she won Studio One, the national song-writing competition. She'd entered it under a fictional man's name. It was 1967. She didn't believe the judges would award a prize to a woman. We kids came home from school at lunchtime for a special dinner with my grandparents. We all had a sip of this unknown drink, champagne, the first alcohol my mother had ever bought.

My father found out. His views on abstinence from alcohol were a guiding force in his life. No one drank in our family. No one mentioned alcohol. Especially, no one brought it into the house.

Yet this era was also the forefront of feminism, and a woman's right to choose her own values. It was a clash of deep convictions. A conflagration.

For years I carried that fraught day with me, until I came to understand, through my own failings and frustrations, how fear of change, fear of loss, fear of the unknown, and fear of the urgings of your own unlived life, can drive a person to act.

I don't know what Dad thought or felt about that time. I didn't ask him, and nor did my mother, nor did he ask her. And so, as often, we all continued in the wake of events interred and unexplained. I had the warm fur of my cat Tunku to hold on to. He smelt like leather and summer grass.

Eventually my parents divorced. We lost our home with the fruit trees and the willow and our father, and Gypsy in the paddock by the plaster factory down the road, and my grandparents around the corner. That search for a place to call home, for a place to be the person I am, began then, and ends here, in the straw-bale house.

I think my mother and father had great gifts to share with each other, if they had appreciated the gifts the other brought. What we most desire, the German philosopher G.W.F. Hegel proposed, is to be recognised as an equal by an equal other. From this state of mutual recognition of 'what each other essentially are in themselves' arises unity. They both remarried – Dad to his badminton partner, Mum to a man who loved singing – and both had more children and long, fulfilling, companionable and respectful marriages. Perhaps they married the wrong person at the start. Or perhaps the wisdom that leads to gratefulness, equality and respect came later in their lives, as it often does.

CHAPTER 3

A Patient Teacher

The plan for a house is a spell that takes physical shape in the future. Here the ideas are cast for something that will arise in macrocarpa beams and concrete foundations.

During 2011, I lived in Wellington to finish my Master's degree. I sat at a desk in my friend's apartment, where I looked out over the railway station and Parliament buildings, and tried to imagine a house, sketched on paper, where the sun would rise over Rough Ridge and set on Blackstone Hill. I planned how I would fit my children and grandchildren in when they came home together.

My son Nick and his fiancée, Bex, sat down with me for an afternoon of sketching. We worked busily at our plans, going through pages and pages of paper. That we could do this, make up designs with our pens, that would be built with hammer and nails, seemed perfectly normal, and by doing it together made it seem more real. If they believed, then my dream was true. It was as simple as that. Drawing a picture that would manifest itself on earth.

What I drew and imagined then, I would one day live in, and pay for. And knowing now what those costs became, I could perhaps have gone for something as small and simple as a one-roomed hut again. But hindsight is a wonderful thing and doesn't help when resource consent needs to be procured and a plan of the house provided.

Not really knowing what was involved in building, what scale things would be, I gave my sketches to the architect, Grant Harris. The cottage I drew looked like a miner's cottage of old, with a loft under the high-pitched roof. The architect's plans improved on mine, with sliding corner windows to look out on the mountains. An engineer was brought in to ensure the house would go through council, with all beam work ticked off. And the house sailed through its permits.

People often ask me, *How did you get on with the council?* And I am able to say the council stamped the house through, first go; in less than two weeks the permitted plans arrived in my mailbox. The sketching and planning took maybe four months, the negotiating with the architect another three, the engineer a month, the council two weeks.

And now there is a strawbale house, with a seat outside the front door, beneath the kitchen window. I look across a small enclave of vegetable garden to apple trees in blossom, and then the hills and rocky tors of Rough Ridge, where often mist hangs about the boulders, and unseasonable snow sifts down on the crest like sugar. I lean my back into the rough plaster of the walls, warm in the morning sun, and think of all the hands that pressed this coat into the house. Over to the left, beyond the small stream, a hawk rides the thermals, wings outstretched, moving in slow circles, as if there is a meal down there in the seeded grass.

In my life up north at the beach, there weren't hawks. Starlings were rowdy every morning at dawn, and oystercatchers flew over the house from the sea, calling out, long lonely sounds as they flew inland to feed. At the farm cottage, a tui used to come and gorge in the plum trees amongst the froth of white blossom, dipping the branch with its weight, and flying away, heavy and low, its white throat feathers shining.

Here in the Ida Valley, the hawks are predator brown and their cruising in the sky an ownership of territory, and what they think of us below, who believe we own the land, we cannot know. We're just creatures like them, who place ourselves at the centre of the world.

Frost came early into the building project, and even snow, in January 2012, five centimetres of white over a summer landscape. When it was minus eight in April I walked to the general store, hat clamped on my head, and exclaimed about the temperature, and the shopkeeper Rhonda smiled at me and said, 'Well you wait till it's 20 below.' When it was almost 20 below in July, we had snow half a metre thick, and when it melted, my land from the first stream to the hills was one sheet of water. In the night the wind raged against the western side of the house, hitting and dissipating into the thickness of the walls. The plan and the engineer's reckoning and the cranking down of the straw bales and the thick hand-plastered layers of mud all stood up to it; wind, rain, sleet, snow and days of baking sun.

'The hardest part of building a house is getting it out of the ground,' Sam told me. And that's because all else is built on the foundation. If the pad isn't square, the walls won't be square. If the pad isn't a sound structure, what is built above it won't be safe. Sam had taken great care setting up the string lines and the profile boards, which gave us the straight angles for digging in the trench. All was well with new beginnings.

Sand came next for the pad. The local trucking company, Beckers, sent it up the road by the scoopful in the JCB backhoe loader. When the piles were dumped, Sam and I raked under the hot sun, smoothing out the piles. There was blue sky above us, and in the willows sparrows chirped. White cloud foamed over Mt Ida, the blue shouldery mountain that rises beyond the pines at the end of my paddocks. I pushed the rake away on the hot, gritty sand and pulled it back towards me, levelling out the humps.

There was something about smoothing the surface of the sand that satisfied. If digging the foundations for the house was an act of going deep, literally turning over things to begin a new life, then raking the sand out level seemed a symbolic act of making sure all obstacles had been taken care of.

We'd hired a small compactor to compress the sand. Sam walked slowly up and down in straight lines holding the vibrating machine while I raked. It looked a difficult job to control the compressor, but I'd made a decision to do everything on site, and use every machine. I took my turn. The rotating steel pulsed and glided over the sand. It was a form of mindfulness, staying aware to guide the machine and keep it moving forward. It was my first instance of realising that power tools that seemed large, unwieldy and difficult to operate were not necessarily so. It only takes concentration to operate anything. Some tools take more strength, but every day on the building site I became stronger and stronger, just by the fact of being there and doing whatever needed to be done.

The first 'building' job Sam had given me was in the first week of the project, in November, when he showed me how to use a drill to put screws in the foundation boxing. He'd instructed me how to press hard with the correct angle and didn't comment when five times, six times, ten times the drill slipped, the screw fell out and I'd have to start again. If he hadn't been so patient and non-judgemental about my first attempts, I could have been shamed. He just said, 'You'll get it eventually,' and told me to lift my hand up so the drill was at the correct 90-degree angle. And then I did get it. Using the power drill to put in screws became one of my favourite jobs on the whole project, simply because it reminded me how far I had come.

Four months into it, in February, I volunteered to do all the cutting for the roof joists with the drop saw. A builder friend of mine had lost his hand in a drop-saw accident. It only takes a moment of distraction for things to go wrong. I thought

A patient teacher, Sam, and the house framed up behind us.

of Bill often. It helped me stay aware, to make sure one hand pressed firmly on the timber to be cut and that at all times I knew where the blade was spinning.

I learnt there isn't an invisible line where on one side there are power tools and practical skills and on the other side unskilled people like me who have to rely on others to get practical things done. It's just a matter of time and practice, of someone having the patience to teach you (or failing that, Google will). And all things can be learnt. Some things take longer than others, and a lot of that is to do with the teacher and how much we desire to learn something.

My fourth form sewing class at Palmerston North Girls' High School was a disaster for me (and probably the teacher). The A-line skirt that was supposed to be completed by term one took me most of the year. The whole business was so stressful: translating the pattern, operating the machine, threading the machine … The teacher with her stout stockinged legs and bulky frame would stand over me exasperated as she told me once more how to do it. She'd give up on my wavery sewing lines (a rapidly accelerating machine) and go to the girls who had finished their skirts and were on to making pyjamas. For them sewing was a swimming pool of water they dived in and swam length after length, while I was still figuring out how to get out of the changing room.

The sewing machine and the tissue patterns were all too much and I gave up trying. My stepmother Jenny made another attempt to teach me to sew an A-line skirt when I was 16. But it wasn't until I was 20 with my own small daughter who needed dresses and tops that I decided I *had* to learn to sew. If I couldn't read patterns or work electric machines I would teach myself my own way.

I bought an old treadle sewing machine, cut shapes out of material and simply sewed them up, trundling my feet on the treadle at a sedate pace instead of the hysterical bursts of power from an electric sewing machine. Soon I had cotton tops with gathered necklines and sleeves.

When I had confidence I bought a pattern and figured that out. I went on to sew shirts for my husband, my own dresses, patchwork quilts. In the years of little children and no writing, sewing became my creative outlet. It was by first making something that I needed, and using the most basic equipment, I learnt a practical skill and went on to master it.

Sam didn't know any of this when he took me on as his apprentice – my basic inability to figure out tools and machines or how to read instructions. His patience and repeated encouragement on that first day working together gave me the confidence to keep trying, to keep learning. No towering sewing teacher now to put the fear of failure into me.

For the concrete pad, once the sand was compacted and level, the plumber, Quentin McFeat, drove over from Queenstown to lay the pipes that would emerge from the concrete pad. This would keep the drainage and water lines safely in the flooring and not in the strawbale walls. I'd chosen Quentin to be the plumber because he'd worked on strawbale houses before and, in fact, lived in one, which he'd invited Sam and I to come over and inspect. He and Sam had worked on building sites together over the years, and Quentin, like Sam, had a young family to support. I was glad to give him the job. His quotes came in reasonably, and now that I had the chance to meet him, I liked the way he talked, with that slow drawl of someone who has learnt what is important in life. Much later in the project, I was the recipient of his kindness.

The plumbing went in and we spread black polythene on top of the sand and buried pipes. When it was time for the polystyrene sheets for the floor pad, Sam asked me to cut one. I took one of his pencils, his tape measure and the saw. The sheet fitted perfectly.

'That's great,' he said. 'Go and cut me three more that size.' Each time I carried him the cut sheet and walked back to the trailer, the builder's pencil in my pocket, I felt a surge of joy. The sun shone, the grass spread out green around the building site, and over the sound of birdsong, the Ida Burn rushed over stones. I could measure. I could be the apprentice that could do the task the builder asked. I liked doing something where preciseness mattered, where I could measure the exact mark to put my pencil line, and everything would work out.

We fitted all the polystyrene sheets over the black polythene by early afternoon, the breeze being particularly kind to us. Carrying the big sheets would not have been fun in a nor'wester. Next step then was the steel. A truck had delivered a pile of reinforcing sheets and a pile of other steel shapes that Sam called starters. And there were long rods. I didn't know what anything was for, but as it is with building, in time everything makes sense and is mastered.

What the odd-shaped steel pieces were for was to construct cradles of steel for us to hang down into the trench we'd dug for the perimeter of the house. The trench would hold the extra depth of concrete that would be poured into it, providing strong footings for the house and all the timber work above the trenches: the heavy macrocarpa beams, the straw, the roof and the windows. If there was ever an earthquake, the steel reinforcing in the trench would help protect the house from lateral movements.

We laid two long rods of steel between two sawhorses, and then worked our way towards each other hanging the square-shaped pieces of steel, the starters, on the steel rods. When we finished one section we carried the rods over and lowered the whole cradle into the trench. When all the trenches were done we began to carry the big mesh sheets of reinforcing steel to lay them on the polystyrene.

Each sheet of reinforcing took all my strength to lift from the ground and then to hold above my head. We walked across the grass and carefully onto the polystyrene. I had to be strong, too, to bend down and lay the sheet in place, covering the white polystyrene with the squares of rusted steel. The sun had gone behind clouds by now and the late afternoon breeze was cold, which made manoeuvring the steel tricky.

We were up to the last sheet to place. I had to brace myself to pick it up. Sam seemed indefatigable. When a job needed to be finished, he pressed on and on, not flagging, not complaining. He'd told me that on site it's much better for everyone if people keep up a good energy, not whining or slacking, because that helps each person to keep going.

'Last sheet, you're doing great,' Sam said. I took a deep breath, bent down and picked up the steel. *Come on arms, you can do it.* Sam led and I followed, holding the sheet above my head. But my arm strength gave out on me. The minute I faltered, the weight of the steel came down towards my shoulders, and straight over

Preparing the floor pad under the Otago sky.

my head, which fitted into one of the square-shaped holes of the mesh. Sam kept walking. I staggered after him holding the sheet as best I could in the gusts, with my head sticking out of it.

'Sam, Sam,' I called. 'My head is stuck.' But he couldn't hear me in the wind. We stepped up onto the polystyrene and over to the last gap, where we would then drop it.

'Sam!' I screamed out and he stopped and looked back at me.

'You're all right,' he said, and waited while I lifted the sheet up over my head again, then we dropped it into place.

It seemed an endless day, and I stumbled in a rut walking back to the caravan. I'd parked the caravan by my shed, a hundred metres from the building site, in a more sheltered site. We had no running water or power and all the jobs ahead of me seemed too much as well – carry water from the tap, cook tea out of something on the gas primus stove, or even get changed. Sam began making tomato soup and I took off my boots and jacket and lay down exhausted on my bed.

'That was a great job, today,' said Sam. 'I didn't think we'd get that pad fin-ished all in one day. Good work.'

The phone rang and he went outside to say goodnight to Indy and Phoenix. I thought of Hana at home in Queenstown, coaxing the little ones to bed in the late summer light.

We were all ready for the concrete truck to arrive. Because my house was small and almost an hour from the concrete firm's base, we weren't a priority for them and had to wait our turn. As the foreman said to me, it's more cost effective to travel and do a big job than to come to a small job like this. So Sam took some days off to go to Queenstown to be with Hana and the children, and I spent the days planting fifteen heritage fruit trees, mostly apples and some plums, along what would one day be my drive.

I told Rhonda Campbell at the store that I was planting fruit trees, and she said, 'More with hope than experience.' She told me they sometimes go four years without any fruit on the trees in the district. Not my tough heritage trees, I thought, but sure enough, later on in spring, a fierce frost hit my trees when they were in full blossom, and once again, trees around the district didn't bear fruit that season.

On a fine Monday morning the concrete truck trundled onto the site. The grey concrete slid down the chute and over the top of the steel that covered the poly-styrene, that covered the black polythene, that covered the sand, that covered the scraped dirt and the trench we had laboured over. In an hour the concrete build-ing pad was all smoothed over.

What remained was for Sam to chalk out the rooms on the hardened concrete floor and I was to prise off the foundation boards and de-nail them.

Before the project started I'd proudly bought myself my own hammer from the building supply shop. I'd bought a toolbelt off Trade Me; a simple, worn leath-er pouch on a leather belt. When I told the seller I was going to use it while build-ing my house in Central Otago, she said the belt had been her father's, and that it was returning to the area where her father had spent most of his life. I thought of that father, perhaps like my own father, careful with his tools, tidy with his mate-rials, his attention on doing a good job.

I walked over to the pile of boards Sam had yanked off the concrete. Beside me, on the foundations all done and true, the chalked shapes of walls and spaces began to appear. Now at last I had a hammering job. I buckled on my new toolbelt and pushed the hammer through the loop.

CHAPTER 4
Staying Connected

I drove back into Central Otago in January, after a break from building to be at my son Nick's wedding in Wales. My car was the only car on the road. I drove into a sunset that lit the hills and rocks with golden hues. Closer to the Ida Valley the Hawkduns flared with pink light.

In Wales, daughter Evie and I had had to negotiate roads crammed with cars, even though we passed through such beautiful villages. The stone houses, pressed up to the footpaths, almost made us cry. It was the simplicity that affected us, I think, and the sheer number, whole streets full, of homes all hewn from stone and made by hand.

Everywhere we went in the United Kingdom, it seemed humans had imposed their vision – in buildings, factories, churches, homes; in cultivated fields and lowland hills severed by fences. There the earth did as it was bid, to a certain extent, although nothing can stop the rain now.

Here, in this much emptier country, and especially in Central where the sky reigns, and then the mountains, and the hills and the rocks, the scale of what humans do is different.

Yet change is happening; the golden tussock lands turning to the bright green of rye grass on the other side of Blackstone Hill. Pivots spurt water from the Manuherikia River onto land for dairy cows. The cows' dung and nitrate-laden urine and the fertilisers needed for green grass are doing what we don't know yet to the underground water systems we all in the end rely on: ducks, hawks, gulls, sheep, trout, householders, and the children who wish to swim in rivers.

The Merino sheep clustered in their dusty paddocks, their wool the colour of the hills, still rule this side of Rough Ridge and long may they do so. The farmers out on the hills in the early morning with their dogs, and the lines of sheep dissecting the slopes, their cloven hooves lighter on the soil, their rattly dung rolling into rock crevices.

As for our own waste, from day one of the build, Sam and I had to become acquainted with buckets. Across the world, the bucket system, known as the humanure system, after Joseph Jenkins' book, *The Humanure Handbook – a guide to composting human manure*, is making life biologically safer where there is no sewerage system, especially in post-earthquake areas such as Haiti, where many schools and orphanages run the bucketing toilet system. The rudiments of it are:

- one large bucket, like a nappy bucket with lid
- a cheap toilet seat to put on top; otherwise, use the bucket's lid for closing it
- a bucket full of carbon-based material: junk mail works fine, and rejection letters. (In Haiti they use the by-products of sugar-cane production.) Here, untreated sawdust is an easy solution. A friendly timber mill can provide a cheap or free supply.

And the process is:

- Step one: Use the bucket.
- Step two: Sprinkle with sawdust and close the lid. Surprisingly there is hardly any smell.
- Step three: When the bucket is full, tip it into a compost bin that is able to be covered with more carbon material such as straw. Leave for 12 months.

Toilet situation solved.

The bucket system worked fine for us for three months and then the septic tank was put in on the house site. Because the house is on a raised, stony area of land, an exploratory dig had shown I only needed the most basic of septic tanks, plus two 20-metre-long diffusion ditches. Sam Forsyth of Black Dog Digging did the job for me. All up the septic system cost $14,000. If I had had to put a system into boggier land, that figure could have been $25,000 or more.

For a toilet, Sam knocked us up a three-sided structure out of old corrugated iron with a timber pallet for a floor. That seemed luxury, especially when Sam made a door for it at my insistence. Here you could sit and look at the stars at night, or gaze across the paddock to the willows. I could surreptitiously check my phone in the middle of a building day for a few minutes out of the hot sun and sight of the boss.

When the toilet went up and I was first to use it, a rock exploded in a crash against the wall. I screamed. Sam said it was a ritual on building sites. The men always did it to each other. I thought I would get my own back and a few days later I picked out a rock, waited for Sam to settle down inside, then hurled the rock at the toilet. Unfortunately my aim went wide, Sam chose that moment to step out of the toilet and was nearly clocked in the head.

I tried one more time a week later, with the exact same outcome, nearly knocking the precious builder out. After that I decided I didn't have the aim to be safe for Sam and would have to forgo the pleasure of getting him back. He kept up his stone throwing, sporadically, and I never got used to it.

The joys of the outside toilet began to pall as winter crept on us. In minus eight-degree frosts you almost stick to the freezing toilet seat. And what's more, the water is frozen in the toilet. On the coldest mornings we'd walk down the road to the public toilet. On snowy, windy nights it was off-putting to get up in the night and go out in the dark to that chilled seat. But on starry nights, the trip held unexpected pleasures, the night sprinkled with galaxies.

At the Museum of New Zealand, Te Papa, there is a Maori whare you can crawl in and sit around the pit of a glowing (electric) fire. You can imagine how it was to live in this way, where a house was a place you crawled in to sleep side by side with your family, your breaths joining together under the low roof.

You can go into the houses, too, in the restored Chinese village in Arrowtown, where the tiny stone cottages of the Chinese miners have been reconstructed along the banks of the Arrow River. It's one of my favourite places to take Indy and Phoenix, not just for their delight in the child-sized doors, but for my own enjoyment as well. I like to stand inside the cool, stone room beside the stone fireplace and the one glassless window and imagine a bed and table and food cooking on the fire. A home constructed from the elements of the earth, and a few yards along the track another home and a few yards past that, another, all in sight and sound of the crisp Arrow.

In the gold-mining days, the slopes and flats around the tiny houses were planted in vegetables to feed the miners. Today we live in houses that trap us with screens we stare at, with traffic to negotiate to procure food, and an overwhelming number of work hours needed to pay for our rooms. If there are rivers nearby, they cannot be heard from our doorsteps. One day, and maybe not so far into the future, we will have to live again simply and in accordance with what we can share from the earth. The rivers' needs, the sky's needs balanced against our own. Which are what? Warmth, shelter and sustenance. And our tribe nearby.

When I was living and studying in Wellington, that first year on my own in 2011, as well as drawing up plans for the strawbale house, I had to try and find a builder. From my teaching of mythology, I knew that once you started on a journey and made the first steps in commitment, you stood at the threshold of a new world. There were tests in this world, and I'd already had several major ones, not the least where to live. I didn't think of Sam to be my builder then. He'd never worked with straw, and he was still in his adult apprenticeship. What's more he had a busy family life in Queenstown with Hana, little Indy and new baby Phoenix.

I was going to build in a place where I didn't know anybody. I didn't know the tradesmen or who to trust. I wanted to help build my house, but the first builder I contacted, before I even said he had the job, took over from me and began organising contractors, the sewerage guy, the engineer for the plumbing design, the roading quotes.

My budget for the house was tight. I had $240,000 from the sale of my beach house, and almost $100,000 of that had gone in buying the land and costs for a year at university. An Auckland friend, when I said I needed to build a house for under $150,000, told me I was so underfunded I shouldn't even start. But I knew Hana and Sam had built their little house in Queenstown for this the year before, so I believed it could be done.

This first builder who went about getting me quotes hadn't taken heed of my budget. Suddenly I had a quote of $40,000 to build an access road in, and this was so out of my reach – a quarter of my building budget – that I began to feel as if the project was spiralling out of my control before I'd even begun. I went into finding a builder naively. I didn't know who to ask questions about his suitability. I didn't take charge with authority when I spoke to him on the phone.

I went down to Queenstown to stay with Hana and Sam and the grandchildren, and Sam overheard me talking on the phone.

'That builder's walking all over you,' he said. 'You have to talk firmly to him. Don't talk like you're scared of him.'

'But I almost am.'

'People will boss you this whole project unless you start talking like you know what you want and you mean it. Don't apologise in your tone. Be adamant.'

'Ok.'

'Practise with me now,' Sam said.

'Um, ok.' I mimed picking up a phone. 'Hi, I'm ringing up to ask you if you can send those quotes on to me from the plumber. And can you give me the name of a referee who you've built a house for?'

'You sound like a young girl,' Sam said. 'You sound like you're asking a favour of him. Take charge of it.'

I deepened my voice, pretended I was a builder in my work boots with tool-belt on my hip, stopping in the middle of a busy worksite to get onto that bloody contractor.

'Hi, listen, I need that plumbing quote by Friday. Thanks. And can you email me two names of people you've built for. I'm not making any decisions till I've checked out a few things. Cool, ok. I'll get back to you in a few days.' I blew my cheeks out. 'How was that?'

'That was good. Keep that up. Now ring him up for real.'

'Now?'

'Yes. And keep your voice deep like that.'

Hyped up on bravura I rang the builder back. But he didn't answer.

It helped me if I understood my strawbale building project as a quest, with all its attendant allies and enemies, the Shadow, which is mostly fear of the unknown, and the mentors who would arise when I most needed them.

In mythology, when a hero sets out on a quest, after he's overcome his own doubts and committed to the journey, the first thing he faces are the threshold guardians. These are the obstacles put up to challenge you – how much do you want this journey? Do you have the determination to see it through? Threshold guardians can take the form of weather holdups, vehicle or tool breakdowns, ill health or lack of finance, the undercutting of your confidence by a friend or stranger, or tasks that seem impossible to do at the time. Sometimes in myths it's a family member, like Theseus's grandfather saying to Theseus, *Don't go*, when Theseus wanted to set out and find his father.

When you set out to do something radically different, a fearful leap into the unknown, there are always people who will say *Don't do it, don't go* ... The task is to sort out what are genuine warnings to take heed of and what are challenges you need to overcome to do what you desire.

Obtaining a builder was another set of guardians to pass. How much did I want this house? How strong could I be when it came to dealing with people? Was I going to let myself end up with someone who didn't listen to what I asked for? One thing I knew for certain, I could not afford a $40,000 road. I was not going to let a stranger accept quotes and organise jobs out of my price range or my home would be in jeopardy. I had to toughen up.

Getting a builder for a house is one thing, but one who had experience in strawbale houses was trickier. The ones who had worked on them were booked up. The ones without experience didn't want to take the project on. And who would want a grandmother as their only labourer? Again I was faced with a decision: should I just take on a builder to build a conventional house, bringing their own team of workers, or should I scrap everything and buy a ready-made house?

This was my chance, though, perhaps my only chance, while I still had strength and good health and the will to learn how to build. I *would* get past those threshold guardians of fear.

I was told about a strawbale building contractor further south. He would watch over the process, keep all tradesmen and contractors on schedule and inspect their work. He would make sure all bills were paid on time and consent inspections arranged. He would take over the project; he would make my strawbale home happen. This seemed like a relief at first. Then hitches began to appear. I still had to find my own builder, and this man would monitor the builder and everything else – for a price.

I can see that for someone busy and with money, a project manager is one way to have a house built. The bottom line is, I didn't have the almost $20,000 he was asking for, to take care of things for me. This time I was firmer. I said no. Back to finding a builder.

After watching me struggle with builders, Hana and Sam made me a proposition. Once I finished university at the end of 2011, if I lived with them for six to eight months and helped with the children while Sam built their next house, he would then come over to my property in the Ida Valley for three nights a week. For $30 an hour he would build my house, with me as his labourer.

'But you haven't built a straw house before,' I said to Sam.

'You've got plans,' he said. 'We'll be able to figure it out.'

My permits were all ready to go. I was close to getting a home again if I found another builder right then. Could I share a room, and a bed, with my granddaughter, could I put my independence on hold to have the chance to work with family, to run the project with Sam helping me every step of the way, and to do what I originally believed in with all my heart – that anyone is capable of building their own home?

It was an easy choice. I said yes.

A few years later, when I was finally living here in the house, I stayed a few days each week with Hana and Sam to help them on another building site. I went back to sharing a double bed with a sleeping child (this time with Phoenix, three years old).

'How did we all fit in here for so long?' Hana said. There'd been five of us in an

80-square-metre house with two bedrooms. Back then, Hana had been running her social media business, I was working on my thesis, and Sam was completing his adult apprenticeship as a builder.

Before we settled into work at night we'd share the family duties. I took turns bathing Indy and Phoenix or cooking tea. Hana and Sam read stories and put the kids to bed and I tidied the kitchen and sitting room. In autumn, Sam went out on his mountain bike foraging for fruit and at night I showed Hana, the way my mother had shown me, how to prepare and boil the fruit, how to overflow the jars and upend them on the bench, rows of glowing apricots and pears, to help them seal. Then we got on with our work, Sam and I with our books spread over the kitchen table, Hana at the computer.

I didn't know anyone else my own age in Queenstown, I had no new friends to visit or have coffee with. I no longer had a partner. But I trusted at some point in the future I would meet new people and move into my own life.

Sometimes when up town I'd look at couples as if they were a strange species I didn't understand. I'd look at men I passed on the streets, and ask myself, would I like this one? Or this one? How would I know? How would I trust a man? How would I meet one? I'd go into cafes alone, armed with a book or my journal and pen and sink into the comforts of coffee and music and people around me, then go home to a skinny-armed hug from Indy or Phoenix.

I'd made a deal with myself that I wouldn't get involved with anyone for at least two years after the breakup. I wanted to make sure I'd sorted out my own contributing behaviour (a life-long task) and learnt to be independent. After 37 years of two marriages, I had to learn how to rely on myself, not, as Sam pointed out to me, always relying on a man to shelter me or do things that needed to be done.

Those months when I lived in Queenstown, where we became a unit that cared for each other, were precious. We gave each other space and quiet to get on with our own projects, even if we were only an elbow-space apart. It showed me how it is possible to live like this – in small spaces, in layers of generations, and in moments of happiness.

When I had to pack up my home in 2010 and put everything in storage, not knowing how or when I would have a home again, I cried over packing up the doll's house. I didn't know how to be the person I was if I didn't have a place or belongings that were mine. And I learnt, as I imagine anyone does who loses a home through storm or fire or loss of any kind, that nothing stops you from simply loving. Time with the people you care about is all that is important. I became, for the next ten months as it turned out, simply 'Grandma'.

CHAPTER 5

All but the Kitchen Bench

It was already late in the summer, February 2012, and Sam had asked me several times, *Have you got the straw sorted yet?* I had two problems to solve with the straw: one, where to find 350 bales of the right size that were dry and baled tightly, and two, where was I going to store the straw till I needed it for building, seven months away?

There was a bale of straw outside the local plant nursery. I started there and asked where they bought their straw from. From a farmer who had specially baled it, they said, and they had bought the entire crop. This is when I learnt that farmers don't make small rectangle bales as per usual anymore. They mostly pressed bales three times the size. Any runs of small bales needed to be organised in advance. I didn't know any farmers and there certainly weren't any grain farmers nearby in Queenstown. And the season was almost over.

I rang a strawbale building company but they said they didn't know of anywhere to get straw. I googled straw suppliers and came up with companies who had the large-size bales or who didn't reply to emails or phone calls. Ah, but what about Trade Me? I put 'straw bales' into the search and up on the screen came seven farmers.

I emailed the three nearest Central Otago, and one farmer emailed back promptly with a phone number. Yes, they still had straw standing. Yes, they would specially bale 350 bales for me as tight as the machine allowed. And yes, they would safely store the bales for me all winter for a small price. When I got off the phone I went out to the sitting room and high-fived Sam. I had my builder and now I had the bales.

Once the straw had been baled, Sonia and Mark Dillon, the farmers, invited me to come over and inspect the bales before I paid for them. It was a two-hour drive from Queenstown to the farm out of Gore. Sonia took me in her four-wheel drive, her two children in their carseats, up through the farm to a high hayshed beside a copse of pine trees. There was the straw, golden and dry.

'Where was it grown?' I asked Sonia, and she pointed out the land behind the shed, now newly ploughed, the furrows a rich chocolate brown.

I imagined for a moment the barley still growing there, the light like quicksilver on the heads of grain. In the shed, beside the stacked up bales, I pressed my hands against the slinky stems of straw that would become my walls.

With the house being built from natural materials, Sam and I decided it would be best to keep the non-toxic process throughout the framing as well. Quentin McFeat, the plumber, had told me of a man, Chris Cox, who had a small timber mill, Puketapu Timbers, in Palmerston, about an hour away from the Ida Valley. Chris specialised in providing naturally durable timber for projects such as mine.

In June of 2012, I called on Chris with my friend Declan Wong, who was filming the strawbale project as a record for the helpers and family. Chris, a tall, rangy man with a welcoming grin, took us to a small hut, an old railway cottage, which was his office, and though it was my birthday and he didn't know it, he served us real coffee and fresh muffins and spent the better part of an hour discussing the project and his love for timber.

'What made you get into the timber industry?' Declan asked Chris.

'I grew up in Wanganui,' Chris said, 'with an old pine forest over the back fence. My mother would say *Get out of the house you children, and don't come back till teatime.* All of us kids in the neighbourhood spent our childhood in that forest. We climbed trees, made huts, lit fires, yeah not so good. There was a big old gum tree and wattles. I was fascinated by the fungi in the forest. And whenever my father took me hunting in other forests, I wanted to know the names of the trees. My grandfather was a botanist, and I guess I inherited that love of trees. A book that's like a bible to me is Edlin's *Trees, Woods and Man.*'

Chris leaned over and topped up our coffees.

'You know, in a time gone by the foresters were important. Countries were judged by the state of their forests. Beautiful forests. Full of colour, variety, different trees for different reasons. The pine forests we have now are hideous. Industrial agriculture. But I do get to see beautiful old forests on private land, trees the settlers planted. There's a wonderful plantation of 120-year-old oaks at the back of Herbert. And now farm forestry is adding new forests.'

'But is it hard for you to cut down beautiful trees?' I asked.

'What's important is to have sustainably managed forests,' he said. 'Not this scorched earth, 'cut everything down' policy. If we take care of forests, keep planting and taking trees out selectively, we can leave the land and forests in a better condition. In Germany they have a system called Plenterwald, a continuous cover forest, where individual trees are selected to be removed and the forest is always growing. It's an eternal forest.'

We went out to the yard and Declan filmed some of the logs.

'Are these macrocarpa?' Declan rested his hand on a large honey-coloured log.

'Yes, they may even become part of Jillian's house. I'm milling these next week. And over there are a few elm I'm milling for a farmer. A lot of these old runs, the first thing the owner did was plant oak, elm and ash for wheels. The whole system was based around the wheel then.'

'They were thinking long term, planting those trees,' I said.

'They were taking care of the future,' Chris said.

We talked there in the sunny yard with the long, straight trunks around us. Chris's eloquence on the subject of timber spoke of a generosity towards his work. I felt privileged to meet this forester who would mill the trees to provide timber for my house. Like seeing the paddock the straw grew in, I now knew the timberyard and the man who would provide the structure for my walls.

Declan was the first friend I made in my new life. I'd met him through a mutual friend, another film-maker, John Irwin, on my first trip down south after my marriage broke up. Declan is six foot two, half Chinese, part Native American, with long black hair and graceful hands: a sleight-of-hand illusionist and fly-fishing guide as well as film-maker. We discovered we shared a love of storytelling. He'd once had a pet monkey that lived with him on a junk with pirates. I told him about Gypsy, and how she'd attack me if she was free, but when I was on her back would jump anything, full wire fences included. Mostly, though, Declan and I talked about our art. The loneliness of it sometimes. The doubt, especially when you're lost in the quagmire of your fears. Declan was making a film about Twizel, where he lived. I was working on a novel.

'I'm filled with doubt all the time,' he'd said. 'All I want to know is, should this be the way it feels at this stage? Can you talk about the trail of bread crumbs so I can find my way out?'

I could talk about that trail. Only because I'd written seven novels before a publisher accepted one.

'When my third novel arrived back in the letterbox,' I told him, 'I walked out to the clothesline to hang out the baby clothes. I could see my hands with the pegs, the sky behind the singlets, and I could hardly move. I didn't know how I would write another thing.'

'But you did.'

'Not for seven months. By then I had given up all hope of success, of being published. All I had left was a desire to write again. I started another novel.'

'You just keep going,' I said. 'That's the only way I know to get through.'

In my ten-month sojourn as grandmother in Queenstown, our phonecalls concerning the artist's life sustained me. If he ever wanted to build his own house one day, I told Declan, he could come and learn on mine and I would help build his.

In December 2012, six months after meeting Chris at his timber mill, Beckers delivered the stack of timber from Chris's mill: the 4×2s for the framing, mostly untreated Oregon, and all the macrocarpa beams for the rafters, the window framing, the verandah supports. Sam and I stacked it on the concrete foundations, the timber piles wrapped in plastic to protect them from the rain.

'I so appreciate I'll be working with wood that hasn't been treated with chemicals,' Sam said. 'There's no danger of breathing in toxins. I won't have to wear a mask or gloves for protection when I'm sawing it.'

I missed the stage of framing for the inner rooms going up because of Nick's wedding in Wales. He'd said to me, 'Mum, I know by hook or by crook you'll be there.' And so I was.

But I was aware that by travelling to Wales there were things I wouldn't be able to afford straight away for the house. There was nothing structural I could save money on, but a kitchen could be put off till later. I would rather be there with Nick and Bex when they married than have kitchen joinery.

Not long after I made that decision, there happened to be the annual give-away day at City Impact Church near Queenstown. Here people donate unwanted household goods, furniture and clothing. Local firms also donate new materials. Hana and I went with a basket and bags. We'd arrived half an hour late, so most of the furniture outside was spoken for. People sat in the sun on the couches they'd claimed; washing machines and ovens had names on them. We wandered into the hall and looked along the piled-up trestle tables. It was the oddest experience – you could take whatever you wanted. I found cutlery and crockery for the caravan and even a crystal bowl for salads.

Outside the hall, under some trees, sat the donated larger items. I looked at a leather patchwork rug, a fridge, a mountain bike. At the end of the line were two large, brand new stone kitchen benches, one unit with a stainless steel sink in it and the other a matching island bench. They were a shade of greyish brown. Clay coloured, almost. For these you had to put your name on a list. I wrote my name next to number two, my lucky number. I imagined winning them. That's all I'd need for a kitchen – benches and a sink.

Hana was ready to go home by 1.30 p.m. We'd already been through all the books and clothes. There was nothing left to look through. Our bags were bulging.

'We have to stay,' I said. 'They're not drawing the number for the benches till after 2 o'clock.' We sat on the grass and listened to music, along with all the other people who had their names on lists.

A boy won the mountain bike. A couple won the leather rug. The last item of the day was the kitchen benches.

'Mitre Ten generously donated these benches,' said the pastor. 'And the lucky person is … number two.'

Hana turned to me with such a big smile. Probably just like my own. I would have a kitchen.

The weight of the benches meant it took four men to deliver them, and a lot of effort for Sam and his dad Dennis to eventually transport them to my site. Sam thought the benches would be too big for the house and that they wouldn't suit. He thought I should sell them on and he'd help make a concrete bench on site. But I really wanted to keep the benches. I knew once they were in the house I would appreciate every day how, when I had no money for a kitchen, I was given them. And I do.

When we got them to the house we measured the first bench. The kitchen sink was cut into the stone right beneath the kitchen window, as if we had planned it that way.

One afternoon the painter Grahame Sydney, who had heard about my house, called in to look at the construction. He was interested in how this building was being made. His mother's family had all been builders, he told me. We walked around inside the spaces of my house. He examined the structure and asked how I would hang paintings on the wall (into blocks of wood driven into the straw to take nails) as he too was considering straw as an option for building one day. He found the house had an aesthetic beauty and balance to it, with its wide window-sills and quiet walls.

'What colour are you going to tint the lime plaster on the outside?' he asked.

It is his life's business to see things around him in terms of form and colour.

'I haven't thought that far ahead.'

'I'd go for a tussock colour,' he said. 'Something with a yellowy tinge, like the grass on the hills there.'

We walked past where the heavy stone bench was lying on the grass. I told Grahame how I'd won the bench and how the space for the sink fell directly under the window.

'There is a God,' he said.

CHAPTER 6

There's Always a Way

In mythology, once a hero begins a new journey they enter a new world. For me that became the world of the building site. Putting on work clothes in the morning, lacing up boots, strapping on the tool belt – these actions helped transform me into my new role. And when Sam and I drove across the paddock from the caravan to the house site, the van loaded with tools for the day, the first thing either of us did was put music on. Music signalled that work was about to begin. On days when Sam wasn't there and I walked around the site, I missed the loud songs and the sound of our hammers. That was our world: music and tools and timber.

Into this new world come gifts, such as the kitchen bench, and allies, such as Chris, the timber man, Quentin, the able plumber, and Barry Becker, the farmer up the road, who is always generous with his advice and time.

Barry farms 20,000 acres here, on Rough Ridge and Mt Ida Station. He was born in 1942, and has lived here all his life. I don't remember who offered me Barry's name as someone who could give me advice. The first time I rang him he answered, 'Yes,' with a gruff voice. I immediately felt nervous. A busy farmer wouldn't have time for a newcomer on a small piece of land. But making assumptions about people or about anything in a new place, weather included, is not a good place to start. Or, as Barry said to me another time, 'Assumption is the mother of all stuff-ups.'

The second time I rang Barry with questions about my land, he offered to meet me on site. He walked the boundaries with me and showed me where the Ida Burn floods and where was the best place to build, up on a natural raised area, in behind the village. I tried to keep up with him through the long, stalky grass in unsuitable shoes.

'You bloody Aucklanders, coming down here and pushing the prices up,' he said.

'But I'm from Motueka,' I said, before I saw he was cheeking me.

He was right about the building site. When the Ida flooded this year, up over the bridge, the road, and a metre high over a quarter of my land, the house stayed safe and dry.

When Sam and I were putting in the first section of the driveway, Barry came in his lunchtime and helped us with his front-end loader and gravel. On the day when we were retying straw bales to fit in the walls of the house, we ran out of baling twine. I tried to buy a single roll from the farm supply shop. They didn't have the twine I needed.

'Ring Barry Becker,' the man recommended.

I rang Barry. He came down that afternoon. He was dusty, streaked with blood on his cheek ('Not my blood,' he said) and in the middle of treating foot rot on the yarded sheep, but he made sure I had twine when I needed it.

'Well,' he said, visiting me again in the middle of yarding to give me a farm timetable, 'it's good to have other errands to do when it's foot-rot time.'

Barry was just one example of many people in my new community who went out of their way to help me, such as Trevor and Judy Beck, who lent me their shed for storage, Graeme Male, who turned up with his work gloves on whenever he was free, and Zona Averill, a gracious woman, older than me, who loved to build as well. We'd discussed the joys of our toolbelts at a local dinner, and thereafter she turned up on site, dressed elegantly and with gifts of homemade biscuits or soup.

There are obstacles, too, in this new world. The ongoing obstacles of weather, of getting the right equipment and materials on the right day, of the body's limitations (mine, that is, and mostly to do with lack of strength). But trials bring courage. The more trials, the more courage, and that gives you the strength to finish the job.

And when things didn't go right – like the chainsaw fizzing out in the middle of the strawbale process, the electrician pulling out of the job a week before the main wiring needed to be done, or a truckload of timber arriving but not the beam we were waiting on – I learnt to trust that all would work out in some way. The beam would eventually come, another electrician would be found, another chainsaw could be sourced. I would eventually get the hang of what Sam needed me to do. Some obstacles challenged me, and I had to develop skills to get past them.

One day I had to take a load of rubbish to the dump, and it highlighted for me how much I had learnt. I backed the trailer up to the designated dump area (after lots of backing practice getting the trailer onto the house site week after week). I undid the truck strops easily, knowing in myself this was a hard-won skill.

When we were straightening the interior timber framing, Sam had used truck strops to tie two walls together and put pressure on them to straighten. He was up on the top plate and I was on the ground. Sam told me to release the strops and shift them, but I couldn't figure it out. I tried and tried, getting frustrated and hot. What a waste of time it was! Twenty minutes already wasted. If Sam would just stop hammering and come down and do it in one minute it would be a better use of everyone's time.

'I'm not coming down to show you,' Sam said. 'You have to learn how to figure things out. What if you're the only person around? You can't go on in life relying on someone else to do things.'

'Ok!' I said and went back to my frustrated fumblings, until I *did* figure out the release mechanism, and grinned up at him.

That was how Sam was with me. He wasn't my son-in-law or my friend on site. He was my boss, the builder, and I was the apprentice, and I had to keep telling myself that, no matter how tough he was. Would an apprentice whine to his boss that he couldn't undo the strops? Sam stayed firm with me the whole project, always believing I would step up and get things done.

At the dump, once I'd released the strops and curled them up and put them away in the boot, I climbed on the trailer in my cotton dress and sneakers, hoisted up the broken wooden pallets and threw them into the rubbish pit. The man emptying his truck of rubbish next to me glanced over. I had a moment of pride in my level of fitness and my strong arms. I was reminded of how functional a body is if we use it for work. It becomes a body we can trust to get things done, instead of us asking or expecting someone else to be there to do the difficult chores.

The hard tasks began when I arrived back from Wales in January 2013. First day back on site and it was time to get the heavy beams into place. The 250×100 mm macrocarpa beams were stacked on the grass and looked enormous to me. Somehow we had to lift them almost three metres above our heads and attach them onto the verandah poles to support the front and back of the roof. There were only the two of us on site, yet Sam was unperturbed.

'There's always a way,' he said. He bent down to lift the end of the first beam and barely got it off the ground.

'Hmmm,' he said.

Above us the sky was a pale blue in the heat, almost 35 degrees. Mt Ida was a diffuse blue with green highlights on the ridges. A few small clouds near the horizon, and everywhere around us the grass sprang up a fresh and lanky green.

'Do we need to find someone to help us?' I asked, but Sam was already bringing over a sawhorse next to the beam. He managed to pick up the end of the beam and place it on the sawhorse.

'Ok, push,' he said. We began to roll the beam over first one sawhorse then another, till the beam was inside the walls of the frame. Sam lifted one end of the beam again and balanced it inside a frame. Slowly he inched the beam up the wall, then repeated it with the other end, while I balanced it.

'Now, climb up the ladder,' he said. I climbed to the second-to-top rung and put my hands on the beam.

'Are you ready for this?' Sam asked from his ladder.

'Sure.'

At his signal we lifted the beam, reaching it up and up to the verandah posts. The weight was so extreme I thought my heart was going to bust out of my chest.

'Ok, hold it there!' Sam fired a holding nail into his end and scrambled up my ladder and relieved me. First beam done.

'You did great,' said Sam. 'Just five more to go.'

These were probably the heaviest objects I had to lift during the whole building project. We bolted the beam in place and went back down our ladders to repeat the process; three beams along the front of the house, three along the back. I trusted my arms more and more that they could take the weight.

Later on when someone came on site, I'd point up to the chunky macrocarpa timber and say, 'We lifted them all in place ourselves.' But no one else could really know the satisfaction we felt as we overcame the weight and difficulty of those beams.

After work the breeze held off and Sam and I sat, legs dangling on the edge of the concrete pad, to drink a beer. Behind us lay a stack of macrocarpa beams, and in front, the mountains. The radio was off. In the bright swirls of willows all along the Ida Burn sang birds, sparrows, I thought, and blackbirds and starlings.

'How about I get us some hot chips,' said Sam.

'That would be so good,' I said. 'I don't think I could move, not even to cook tea. Thank you.'

Sam lifted his mountain bike off the concrete pad and rode off to the pub.

It had been a long, hard day. My legs felt restful swinging there, nothing required of them. The birds were busy though. There was an orange-breasted bird, a chaffinch, on the fence in front of the small stream of snow melt, and every few minutes it flew up for a feast of midges, then back-flipped like a biplane, to settle on the wire again. A blackbird flew past in a straight line, going places. Two thrushes with chubby bellies pecked in the grass close to the stream. The water must have held all sorts of food, for a white-faced heron landed in the grass and stalked over to wander up and down in the water. For once there were no hawk and magpie bombing escapades. It was only the peaceful birds. Even three quail snickered in a line from the pond to the stand of broom where they lived. On the pond, two grey ducks floated, and behind them, while I waited for chips, the mountains went from blue-grey to pale orange to cerise. My arms ached from the effort of lifting, yet I couldn't imagine tiring of the birds, or the light shows on the Hawkduns and Mt Ida.

The wooden beams were in, but when it came to the steel beam that ran right through the building, we were almost overwhelmed by the task in front of us.

Sam had come up with the idea of using steel to prevent having to use a toxic laminated beam running the width of the house. Beckers had made us a steel plate, 10 metres long, which would be sandwiched between two runs of macrocarpa beams; the whole lot bolted together. We heaved the first set of timber beams up, then began the struggle with the steel beam.

As well as being heavy, the beam was supple yet unwieldy, and it bent in curves as we lifted it. We spent maybe an hour lifting and manoeuvring the beam, and then, for the final push, I sat on top of the wall frame, my legs locked together to hold me upright. Sam stood on the ladder across the room from me.

'Ok, lift,' he said. I grasped the beam and began to lift it but just couldn't raise it high enough.

'I can't hold it, I'm dropping!' I yelled out to Sam. I could feel the beam start to slip through my hands.

'Let it go!' he called back. He couldn't hold his end with the weight of mine coming down. The steel beam crashed to the ground.

The two of us looked at each other and then down at the beam below us.

'What day is it today?' Sam asked.

'Wednesday.'

'Well it should be Twosday. One step forward and two steps back.'

'Should we try and find someone else to help us?'

'No. We can do it,' said Sam. 'We'll just start again and this time use clamps.'

So we inched the beam up the frame all over again. Sam attached the blue clamps at my end and I held the beam in the middle till that, too, was clamped. Twenty minutes later the beam was in place. I took a photo in order to show the building inspector, before we put the next macrocarpa beam up and sandwiched it.

We went over to the cafe across the paddock to celebrate.

'When shall I schedule the strawbale-raising day?' I asked Sam over coffee.

Strawbale-raising days are traditionally when a group of people come together to help stack and compress the straw bales into the frame of the walls. It's a substantial process, requiring lots of strength, humour, agility and forbearance. Having a group of people working together means so much can be achieved at once. In fact, if you have enough people – preferably strong people who know what they're doing – a house could have its straw walls put in all on the one day.

'I don't know when to schedule it,' said Sam. 'There's so much to be done before then. We haven't even got a roof. We have to build the trusses and the roof structure first.'

'But I have to make a date sometime soon. People need to book flights to come.' And definitely we had to have a date so I could book a strawbale expert to help us on the day. I took out my notebook and we listed all the jobs yet to complete and estimated how many days it would take.

'How about March 16?' I said. Winter would come up fast after that. I had to fit a strawbale-raising day in and then a mud-plastering day before the frost and snow arrived.

That night the farmer storing my straw sent me a text: *We need the barn for storing this year's straw. Can you move your straw as soon as possible? Thanks.*

We were months away from being able to bring the straw on site. No roof meant no shelter for the straw, plus we needed the space inside the house to keep building before hundreds of bales could be stacked there.

I asked Brian who I could ask of the farmers around the area and he said, 'Leave it to me.' A day later he came back with an offer from Trevor and Judy Beck down the road. They were retired farmers and had an empty hayshed they were happy for me to use. The shed was close enough that we could make numerous trips with trailers when it came time to use the straw. I found a trucking firm near Gore, where the bales were, and rang them.

'I'll arrive about seven in the morning tomorrow,' the truck driver told me. 'Can you have six or seven men there to help unload?'

Six or seven men? I didn't even know that many people. I told Brian who said, 'Well, I'll come and help.'

Brian – neighbour and building mate. The sun sets over Blackstone Hill.

I rang Beckers trucking firm to see if they had extra men. 'No, we want men ourselves,' the manager said.

At least there was Sam.

'I can't come and help,' he said. 'The roofing timbers are arriving at seven to-morrow as well. I have to be here on site to unload them.'

We woke to the mountains covered with cloud; a sombre, moist grey day. Brian and I are in the yard in the early morning to wait. Right on seven, the double-trailer truck pulled in at the front of the Becks' hayshed. I looked across at Brian. Instead of six or seven farming men to help, here was a poet and a writer. A lean, grey-haired, grey-bearded man, and a grandmother. The truck driver didn't say anything. He climbed on top of the first load and began throwing bales down.

The bales came faster than Brian and I could stack. And I had to watch out. A couple of the bales flung towards me and struck me in the legs so I almost fell.

'Be careful,' Brian growled up at the driver. My back wasn't the strongest and Brian had a shoulder that had been broken twice as well as a crook neck. We just

Early morning in the Ida Valley and the truck arrives with the straw.

kept stacking, sweating now, my heart pumping. The bales kept on flying off the truck, I heaved them over to Brian and he stacked them higher and higher in the shed.

As Brian had said, we must be worth six men any day, and we were. Sam arrived in time for the second load and helped stack that. We did it all in an hour and a half.

Much later, near the end of the building project, when I had to pick up and shift a straw bale, I was so tired I could hardly carry it. And I remembered back to this day when Brian and I lifted and stacked the bales, hundreds of them, and I wondered what strength we had found just because there was a job that needed doing and we were the only ones there.

The straw was safe and dry. Sam, Brian and I went straight to the Ida Valley Kitchen in time for morning tea, before Brian went back to his desk to write and Sam and I to build.

CHAPTER 7

Real Growth

One Tuesday, early in the project, Sam arrived back on site with old louvre windows on the trailer. He'd bought them for $10 at the recycle centre, and that evening set about constructing a small glasshouse attached to the shed where the caravan was parked. Back in Queenstown he had tomato seeds sprouting in containers along the windowsills. The next week, when the glasshouse was ready with pots of compost, he arrived with trays of seedlings, and over the course of the house build, the tomato and capsicum and chilli pepper vines grew.

After a day burdened with a heavy toolbelt and working with steel and timber and machinery, Sam liked nothing better than to drive across the paddock to the caravan, park the van, and go straight into the glasshouse to see to his plants. I'd catch glimpses of him out the caravan window as I cooked dinner, his hands lifted to the rising plants, taking off the laterals, plucking off the excess leaves, and delicately twining the sappy tendrils to string that was nailed from the ceiling.

We had the key to the local swimming pool, the original school pool bought and donated to the community by Alistair Broad and Hilary Calvert when the school closed down. The pool was covered, with its upkeep paid for by community projects. Sometimes Sam and I had enough energy after work to go down for a swim.

'You know,' Sam said one night, as he looked around at the soaring plastic walls of the pool, 'this area would make an amazing glasshouse. All this heat is wasted. People could donate tomato seedlings and take turns watering them. If I lived here permanently, I'd come and look after the plants for everyone, myself.'

Another project he proposed was a community vehicle. 'A diesel van,' he said. 'and then run it on cooking oil from the pub. It recycles the oil while everyone gets free trips to town to do their shopping. And those that go could shop for others.'

'And if that was my front paddock,' he said of mine, 'I'd put communal rows of potatoes in.'

In another small community I'd lived in, Upper Moutere, between Nelson and Motueka, a local farmer had done just that. When we shifted there in the early 1980s, Peter Heine visited us and explained how, for the contribution of a bag of seed potatoes from each household, he would plough the rows and take care of the potatoes. And it happened. At harvest, someone from each family helped to lift the creamy, fresh-skinned potatoes from the soil and took home a sack of potatoes.

But not my front paddock in this climate. Brian and other locals had told me stories of nurturing crops of potatoes with frost cloth on the freezing nights and with water on the hot, dry days, only to have whole crops across the district blasted black, destroyed by a late and unexpected plummet in temperature.

A glasshouse for potatoes? Definitely for courgettes and tomatoes. None of these seedlings that I've planted outdoors have survived yet. In a climate that can produce snow in the middle of summer, gardening here is not for the unwary, as I'm still learning.

Perhaps it is our distance from supermarkets, or some stubbornness in the humans who live here in this startling climate, but people persevere with their home gardens, listening to the weather forecast, trudging out to cover plants in the same way horse owners rug up their animals on a chilly night. A glimpse at the stars showing through after days of rain has Brian saying, 'There'll be a frost in the morning.' And now I, too, look at a rent in a night sky for stars, and think of my new feijoa trees, my newly planted spinach. Anything green or fresh in the garden can mean a meal; can mean one more day without having to go to town.

Nothing can be taken for granted here. In Motueka, everything grew, and everything was safe to grow. Even hops and tobacco grew there, the only area in New Zealand with the right climate and soils. In our little country place in the Moutere we had tangelos, lemons, oranges, grapefruit, mandarins, feijoas, blueberries, pears, and best of all, massive plum trees which, with preserving, gave us fruit all year. At my house where I lived on the beach in Motueka, a sprouted avocado stone I'd planted reached 8 metres in just a few years. Apart from watering, everything grew as if it simply sprang out of the ground, eager to get on with the business of living.

When a neighbour here told me it took 30 years for a tree to be established in the Ida Valley, I thought of the hundreds of natives and silver birches I'd planted further north, that within a few years towered over my head, sheltered tui and offered airborne homes for sparrows. And I wondered when I would have trees again on this place, trees with deep roots in this once ragged and boggy paddock.

I cobbled together a makeshift vegetable garden on the building site, made from sets of six leftover straw bales; rectangles filled with alpaca poo, old straw and soil, and fitted in between piles of wrapped timber. Here grew potatoes, kale, beetroot, silverbeet, lettuces; the leaves bright green amongst the straw. The wind was their foe, and the relentless sun, and the frosts that descended out of the glacial sky. Sometimes pheasants strutted regally across the paddock from the broom to feed on my seedlings, and there were blackbirds and thrushes with scratchy feet. Kale and beetroot, I learnt, are the best garden survivors here.

One night I went to hear atmospheric physicist Greg Bodeker talk in Alexandra about the effects of global warming on our planet. In 2007 he was one of 427 scientists worldwide who shared the Nobel Peace Prize with Al Gore. Bodeker has spent ten years working for the Intergovernmental Panel on Climate Change, his subject, a special report on ozone depletion and its relation to climate change. As much as Bodeker has studied and written and lectured on the subject of climate change, he says the best thing we can all do is go home and grow tomatoes.

'Eighty per cent of my time is spent dealing with esoteric subjects,' he tells me later. 'It's with gardening that I get back in touch with what is real.'

Real is watching the sky for frost, carrying water by the bucket-load. By taking care of plants, I am reminded of the relationship between earth and our own survival.

When it came time to make up the macrocarpa trusses for the roof, Sam and I assembled them over four days, piecing the beams together like a huge jigsaw puzzle on the ground. Under the hot sky we continued working on the trusses, sunblock slathered on the backs of our knees. Sam screwed in the black metal plates to join the beams while I bent over the trusses, hammering nail plates into the golden wood.

Yesterday the road had streamed with sheep. Now, across the road on Rough Ridge, the newly separated ewes called and called for their lambs. Further away, the poignant wailing of the lambs; in between, Sam and I and our tools, and the irrepressible birds.

I straightened up to check my hat was shading my neck and shoulders. The skin on the back of my legs felt hot and tight. I rolled my long shorts down over my knees and calves and unrolled my shirt sleeves. I walked over to the van and refilled my pouch with nails.

The hammer with its warm, leather handle was heavy in my wrist. I used it first with my right hand, then with my left. The steel plate resounded with a satisfying thwank. When I'd gone to buy a hammer, I'd turned down the lighter hammer 'more suitable for ladies' in favour of a weightier builder's hammer. How easy it had been hefting the hammer in the building supply shop compared to when I had six hours of laborious nailing on site. At this stage of the day, the ladies' hammer began to appear desirable.

'Here,' Sam came up beside me. He passed me my water bottle. 'Keep up your hydration.'

I put the hammer down and flexed my wrists.

'What do you think?' I asked. '38 degrees?' A white heat on the hills and the grass seared under our feet. Even the new apple trees had dropped some yellow leaves. Somewhere across the paddocks a tractor growled, turning over earth for winter crops.

Sam and I stood there and guzzled our water. He put Rodriguez on to play, one of my favourites, and we rested there a moment, listening. Amongst the tussocks in the new garden, a red poppy, and then the tawny paddocks topped with white yarrow. The mountains rose up hazy blue beyond the pines.

Sam had made my water bottle. It was a glass bottle he'd wrapped with white electrical tape so the glass wouldn't shatter if I dropped it. On the tape he'd written 'Jillian's Happy Juice', 'Water is Life' and 'Happy Days'. There were daisies and leaves all in blue felt pen; a bottle to make me smile when I was tired.

I looked across at Sam. I wondered if he even knew how much of a mentor he had become for me.

American mythologist Joseph Campbell believes when anyone begins a new journey, 'though life may seem to be endangered by the threshold crossings and life awakenings, protective power is ever present ...' I took comfort in that idea. It meant, by the very fact of taking action, help would be there. 'One has only to know and trust,' Campbell wrote, 'and the ageless guardians will appear.'

I had wondered when my mentors would appear, what form the ageless guardians would take, until I began to see they were already right there in my life.

For a start there was Sam, and when I sorted out the lists of instructions he gave me and his admonishments to be aware, I saw he was teaching me, not just about building, but about taking responsibility for my life and my actions.

At first when he would ask me to go and get something, the skill saw or the ratchet, I'd say *Where is it?* instead of remembering where we stored tools or the last action the tool had been needed for. Or if he asked me to do a task like take the battery from the nail gun and plug it in, I'd immediately say *How do I do that?* without trying to work it out myself. One day, after I'd been rummaging in the back of the van for the small orange crowbar and I'd called out yet again, 'Where is it?', Sam came over to me.

'I've got some advice for you,' he said. 'And everyone needs advice sometimes. Think, and then speak. Or at least look.' He reached into the drawer and lifted out the crowbar, which had been under a tin of drill bits. After that I'd catch myself going to call out questions to him and I'd look again, and look around.

Another day Sam said, 'If I ask you a question, like, have you organised the twine yet, say "Yes, Sam. The twine's coming on Friday." Or, "No, I haven't done that yet." Don't just be quiet because you think you've done something wrong.'

'So I need to have more authority?'

'Yes,' he said. 'With everything.'

One day Sam told me to put some nails in a joist hanger. He looked at the job I'd done and asked me what I thought the point of it was. I looked at the nails I'd banged in any old how in the bracing plate, and shrugged.

'You've missed putting them where they count. What work are they doing?' he asked. 'Before you put any nail in, you have to ask yourself, what function is this nail performing? Know the result you want before you do anything. You don't just do something for the sake of doing it.'

That meant when I hammered in nails in the bracing plates joining one beam to another, I had to get every nail in straight and true. The nails did their work when they went in deep. It became one of my favourite jobs, to hammer in each nail, concentrating, entirely focussed on the swing and angle and weight of my hammer to get each nail in straight.

I clambered over the framing of the house, happily hammering, with my tool-belt round my waist filled with nails. I started to think I was getting pretty good at this building job: able to use a hammer, knowing what all the tools were and how to use them and charge them and where to find them. I was especially enamoured with hammering. A simple task, done as well as I could. How calm and right that felt.

Brian became one of my mentors too. Sometimes just for encouragement and a cup of tea, and other times with his advice to me, be it from his sporting or mountaineering days. Sam often asked me to throw him tools or pieces of timber, or he'd throw tools down to me when he was up on the roof, even the nail gun or a heavy pack of nails. With only two of us on site, invariably Sam up on the frames and me working at ground level, it was quicker to throw things to each other.

'Keep your eye on what he is throwing you,' Brian told me (giving me some sporting advice). 'And when you go to catch it, let it fall into your hands, don't snatch at it. You could damage or break a finger. Bring the weight into your body. That way you're less likely to hurt your hands. When you have to throw something to Sam, keep your eye on him, and follow through towards him with your hands.'

Sam told me when I threw things up to throw them flat, a piece of timber held in the middle and thrown straight up, same for the crowbar or the large spanner. We got so good at our technique that one evening, when I was throwing things up to Sam perched high on the roof, applause broke out. I turned around to see an older couple who were camping at the backpackers next door, sitting in their deck chairs cheering us on.

My confidence in building was about to be challenged, though, when we started working on the roof structure.

CHAPTER 8
Three Points of Contact

In the morning, the wind tugged and whooshed at us as we unloaded the tools from the van. I looked across at the willows, their green branches thrashing. Last night in the south, the sky had been a pale egg-shell blue until late. I turned and looked up at the framing and beams, at the new height I would have to start working from to create the gable roof.

'Is it safe?' I asked Sam, in what would be my catchphrase for the next few months.

'Nothing is safe,' said Sam. That was his reply every time I asked him. 'When you climb up the framing, treat every nog as if it could come loose. Always keep your weight balanced by using your arm strength.'

I hauled myself up the framing onto the first truss beam that spanned the front of the house. Now I had to walk out on the beam.

'It's all about confidence,' Sam called across to me. 'Walk that beam like there's no tomorrow.' Though the fact there could be no tomorrow if I fell was the point of my fears.

My legs felt unsteady, one step at a time. The wind was cold, coming through the empty frames, and it buffeted me as I stepped. I got myself into position to begin hammering nails into the joist hangers in the rafters. I stood on the beam and leant over the rafter to begin, and out of nerves I fumbled the hammer. It dropped three metres to the concrete below.

I looked across at Sam busy nailing in more rafters. There was nothing for it but to go back across the beam and down the frames and then climb all the way back up again. In position for a second time, and being more careful, I leant over the rafter again. Holding the hammer upside down between my second and third fingers, like holding a cigarette, I delicately tapped the first nail at an angle until it was in firm enough to get a good hit at it. Each rafter took two joist hangers and each joist hanger took twenty nails. I manoeuvred my way across the beam to the next rafters.

'Sam,' I called across to him. 'I'm not happy going across this beam.'

'Well, you better get happy,' he called back. 'Because I need you, you're the only one here, and you put your hand up for this.'

I went back to nailing. I didn't know where my confidence had gone. Maybe it was because my lower back ached from lifting timber and my arms and legs were stiff from days of work. I had to concentrate on keeping my head safe from the rafters above me, my legs steady on the beam, and my arm lifting and lifting. Once I was in position I felt ok enough to hammer, but then I'd have to get up and move across the beam again. Fear made my legs wobble.

When I was 16, I'd had a job after school and weekends at a vet clinic in Palmerston North. I took the job because I loved animals, yet one of my tasks, as the lowly young vet nurse, was to bag the dead animals after they'd been put down.

It was like a horror story for me, trying to bend a dead dog's legs to fit in the plastic bag, or tucking a cat's head down to fit in. I was scared to do the chore and couldn't bear to go into the room out the back where the dead animals were. Usually the other nurse would bag animals as well, and even the vets sometimes, but they all decided the best thing for me to get used to it was for me to bag *all* of them. They saved up the dead animals during the day instead of bagging them immediately. I couldn't go home at night until I'd dealt with the bodies. I just had to do it, whatever my feelings were about it. I'd say a small prayer for each animal, being as respectful as I could, thinking, at least I could be that for them.

I don't know why I thought about that job while I was up on the beams. Maybe that when you think you can't do something, you just somehow keep on doing it.

And yet, even up there in the cold, with nervous fingers and shaky legs, there was still that pleasure of hitting a nail over and over, driving it in and moving on to the next one. Life became so simple and clear. I needed the co-ordination of eye and hand, of feet and stomach for balance, and to not think about anything except how to stay safe and hit the nail in.

I thought that was my hardest day on the site. In mythology, a hero moves *towards* their greatest fear, the ordeal where they face their greatest challenge. I thought I had done that. I'd accomplished my job when I was scared to do it and from now on things would be easier.

But the next morning as I walked towards the house site I felt even worse. It was a huge day ahead of us, too. The building inspector was coming and we had to be ready for him. At least there was no wind. No wind, after days of it. It felt instead like frost, the air chilly and the grass crisp under my boots. Mt Ida was a hulking blue and white against the pale sky, and on the tops of Rough Ridge and Blackstone Hill, snow. A prescience of winter not far away.

At breakfast Brian had said to me, 'When you have a lot to achieve, instead of panicking, act with composure. Stay aware, and look and listen.'

I liked that word composure, but as soon as I got on site, my stomach writhed. There was so much to achieve that day. And there were those beams to face again.

Sam asked me to help him shift the scaffolding first. I hadn't done that before. I grabbed the legs at my end and heaved. When I put the scaffold down I accidentally kept my hands where the top legs slotted in. Sam adjusted the scaffold, and the steel leg came down on one side trapping my fingers.

'Ahhhh!' I yelled out and Sam heaved the scaffold leg off my fingers.

'Oh Jillian,' he said. 'You've got to take notice of what you're doing and where you put your hands.'

So much for composure, and for being aware, and looking. The finger that was squashed the most was on the hand I'd broken a year ago, running pell-mell down concrete steps to catch a bus, tripping and falling. Awareness, that's what I needed, and knowing where my body was and what was around me (and how the scaffolding worked).

I looked up at the joist hangers needing nails on the highest rafters, up where I would have no beams to hold on to. I rubbed my sore hand.

'Sam, I can't do those ones up there,' I said.

'What do you mean "can't"? There's no can't on a building site.' He was already up on the scaffold. 'There's the job that has to be done, so you're just going to have to figure it out.'

I climbed the wall of framing up to the truss beams. To go across the truss, I had to climb over one joist, then squat down on the beam and go under the second one. I had to stand up and reach out with both arms wide to go from one rafter I could hold on to, to the next. My boots felt clumsy, my toolbelt was heavy and lopsided with spanner and rachet. That was my first job of the day: tightening bolts where the steel beam and macrocarpa joists met.

I stubbed my foot and stumbled slightly. I got to the next beam then realised I hadn't thought of everything I'd need in my toolbelt.

'Oh no, I forgot the washers.'

Sam looked across at the expression on my face. Agile and entirely at ease on the rafters, he came and brought me some washers from his belt.

'Here you go. Monkey man brought them for you.'

In Sam's previous life, before having children, he and Hana had both been competitive snowboarders. They'd won New Zealand titles for the Big Air, and for Slopestyle, freestyle boarding. Sam had come runner-up in the World Heli-challenge one year. He'd jumped off a narrow ledge high in the mountains and ridden his board down unknown territory, through gullies, between rocks, and down almost perpendicular slopes, the powdered snow like a wave of ice curling beyond his board. He'd said to me once, 'I don't need to take any drugs. I've got adrenalin.'

He brought that same bravery and intense focus to building. And I was grateful for that energy.

Up on the beam I put in the washers and tightened the bolts with the ratchet and spanner. The early sun was already baking the sky a deep blue. On Blackstone Hill, the dusting of snow had melted and the ridges were turning green again.

Then on the last bolt I dropped the spanner. I don't like that clanking sound of a tool being dropped from a height. It also means another trip back across the truss and to the floor. Down the frames I went.

I knew when I went back up I would have to start on the joist hangers high in the roof frame. I looked around first for a plank I could take up there to stand on. I studied the various planks, and the places I could put them. I considered with dread the high rafters and joists.

Sam noticed me standing still on the concrete below him.

'What are you doing?' he asked.

'I'm looking at how to put a plank up there.'

'What else can you do instead? Look around. Do the low joists,' he said. 'It's like the Pac-Man game: clean up the easy points first. We haven't got time for you to be standing around thinking. Keep moving. It's a big day.'

We were under immense pressure because the bale-raising day was set for next week. For bales to go in there had to be a roof on, and to put a roof on we had to have all the roof structure completed and passed by the inspector. He could only come on certain days, and today was the day he could come.

I had to have all the joist hangers nailed in by the afternoon. Sam had to have all the rafters in and the bracing straps on. Or the whole project would be stopped. That would push back the raising day, and then the mud plastering, which covered the straw walls in a protective coat, would end up too far into winter. With

The interminable hammering of joist hangers.

rain and snow, plastering mud wouldn't be possible. The house would have to wait, empty-framed and tarpaulin-protected till spring.

I climbed the ladder and began the lower joist hangers, all the while those high ones were on my mind. I couldn't calm the nauseous feeling in my stomach. The joist hangers were out on a beam where I would have nothing to hold on to.

Before lunch I climbed down and walked to the caravan to make our salad wraps. First I swung my leg over the fence and walked through the pines to Brian's house. I had a cup of tea with him and told him how Sam said there was no such thing as can't on the building site. Brian said his grandfather would say the same thing, *There's no such thing as can't. You have to find a way to do it.*

'Here,' he said. 'You look like someone who needs an orange,' and he brought me a plate with an orange cut into segments on it. 'And remember the rule of three.'

'What's that?'

'That's what we used when we were mountain climbing. Always have three points of contact and you'll be safe, no matter how high you are.'

When I went back after lunch, I climbed the ladder with my toolbelt on and I felt strong again. I felt like I could do anything I needed to do. Where had my fear gone, and what had restored me? The orange and nuts and raisins Brian had given me, or the break away from the site and talking to a friend over a cup of tea?

What's more, when I climbed up, I found if I sat astride the joists I could reach more joist hangers than the ones around me. I felt safe enough to go higher up the rafters. When I had to stand in one point where I couldn't use my hands to hold on, I tipped my head so the edge of my hat braced against the beam, my third point of contact, while I guided a nail in.

I told Sam about the safety of always having three points of contact and he laughed and said *Na, one will do,* and posed high up on the beam on one foot, the other leg and arms in the air. I took a photo to show Brian.

Sam finished nailing on the silver bracing straps that spanned the roof structure in big criss-crosses. It was an hour till the inspector was due. With his own job finished earlier than he thought, Sam came to help me. Monkey man that he is, he sat atop the highest point of the roof and nailed the joist hangers I'd been scared to do.

'I just love heights,' he said. And I was glad he did.

In my new position on the joists I could do the rest of the hangers.

Sometimes, what seems impossible can be achieved – by having a new frame of mind, by trying a new angle, by circumstances changing, such as Sam finishing his job early and being able to help. Or maybe, by having an orange.

The inspector came. I was still up the top, nailing. He walked around talking to Sam and examining our work. When he drove off in the car, Sam gave me a thumbs-up sign and climbed up to join me.

'Two days ago this whole roof structure wasn't here,' he said. 'Yesterday I had my phone in my hand ready to ring the inspector and postpone him. But we just did it.'

I looked up from my perch at the blue sky and a hawk riding the thermals by the stream. We were on track to get the roof on. We were going to make the bale-raising day.

CHAPTER 9

A Roof Over Our Heads

Sam and I were on site when the sun came up. We stopped unloading tools from the van and turned to watch Blackstone Hill light up orange and pink. After three months of building we knew how fleeting the light changes were: Mt Ida translucent in early dawn, late afternoon gilded light on Rough Ridge, and then at the end of the day, on a good day, the Hawkduns and the Ida Range pink as well; a showcase of folds and ridges before dark and starlight appeared.

A few days earlier Sam had said to me, 'You've no idea how much we have to do before the straw bales go in, have you?'

I shook my head. It was Sam who held everything we had to do and the enormity of that task in his head. And the task urgently in front of us now was the roof.

'Well, lack of knowledge is a wonderful thing,' he said. 'You just keep on as you are; stay positive.'

And I did. Every day I pictured the house with the roof on, the bales safely in before winter, even a bench outside in the sun.

Mid-morning, Sam set me up on the grass to fold and roll the building paper that would go under the iron. I rolled the heavy tar paper over the bumpy ground, measured the paper, cut it, then bent and creased a strip each side of it. This would make a channel for any moisture to run safely outside instead of getting into the ceiling.

When he was an apprentice Sam didn't like doing this job, but I enjoyed it. I liked being on the ground after what seemed like weeks of being up on the beams and joists. It was warm in the sun and birds sang in the willows as my fingers smoothed and pressed the paper. For once I had a familiar task, as if the rolls were curtains that I hemmed and sewed. When I was ready with the first creased rolls, I passed four to Sam and climbed the ladder to join him.

'Get ready to catch the paper as soon as it comes near you,' he said from the apex of the roof. 'If the wind catches it, it'll rip, and we haven't got paper to waste. Ready?'

'Yep.' I tightened my legs to balance on the lower part of the roof, hands held apart. He let the roll of building paper go and it uncurled in a rush towards me. The wind snatched at the paper before I grabbed it. I hung onto one corner.

'Hold it down!' called Sam. 'Lean across it, don't let it rip.' He climbed down the rafters to get to me, and made his way up, stapling the paper till he was at the top again. 'Ok, next one. Ready?'

'Yep.'

When we had a quarter of the first part of the roof covered in black, Sam came down and showed me how to carry the long lengths of red roofing iron over to the roof. There I had to prop them against the edge of the building then lift them up, hand over hand till Sam could grab them.

'Think you can carry them?' he checked.

'Sure.' The lengths of iron were heavy and cut into my gloves. I had to hold the sheets in the middle so they didn't buckle and crease. I pushed them up to Sam, and he carried them the rest of the way by himself, stepping up the rafters, with the concrete floor exposed below him. Any weight or discomfort I had on the ground was nothing compared to carrying the sheets while stepping on rafters. What daring, what perseverance a roofer needed to have.

I made a note of what a builder had to be: courageous, for sure. Strong, to be able to get building materials to where they needed to be. Forward thinking, for all the planning that had to go on. Lateral thinking and problem solving, because, as my sometime building mate Brian would quote to me, 'Nothing succeeds as planned.' So far, we were doing good.

I said to Sam, 'Does it make things harder having your mother-in-law as your worker?'

'You're better than most young apprentices,' he said, 'because you understand you don't know the building process, and when I tell you to do a job, you do it, and when I show you how to do something, you listen. You haven't brought any ego or bravado to the site.'

That made up for something. And I did make sure I was biddable. I'd stop doing my job and go and get tools for Sam when he asked. I'd throw them accurately to the roof, keeping my eye on Sam and following through, so he caught his tools easily. I did appreciate how he worked hard and fast, at the same time coaching me along. I know he wished at times he had another builder who could take some of the brunt of the work. I had gone way past the stage of being able to afford another paid helper even if there was a spare builder around these parts.

When we first started building, Sam would come over on Tuesday morning and work through until Friday afternoon. Now with the pressure of the bale-raising day and winter fast approaching, he made the decision to stay on site. We had to get the roof on so the bales could go in, and the mud plaster on before frosts came. That meant working every day without a break. For the roofing we began work while it was still dark and stayed on site after the sun set and we couldn't see anymore.

We'd leave the tools locked in the van and go in and light candles in the caravan. Dinners became as easy as we could make them. Cans of tomatoes heated up with any vegetables we had. Rice, or pasta. No hot bath to relax. It was eat and sleep. Sam in the caravan and me by torchlight to a small tent under the willows.

In the dark of morning we ate fruit and drank coffee in the caravan while we talked through the tasks of the day. Sam made lists of materials by candlelight. Then out by the work van, I cajoled my body to get moving – arms above the head and leaning back to stretch. Buckling on the toolbelt was a sign; here we go again. And once on site, with the sky lightening in the east and the radio on, another day's hard work seemed possible.

On the roof in the day we had a good view of the road, the cafe, the traffic and the locals. Up there in the sun with our music on, it felt like the best job in the world. Sheet by sheet the roof began to sheath the house, creating shade for us below in the 30–40-degree heat.

We knew some of the vehicles that went past, and amused ourselves by calling out to them, even though they couldn't hear us.

'Hey, Shazza!' Sam called to Sharon McKnight who drove the school bus and so would pass us twice a day. We recognised Barry Becker's farm truck and waved and called, 'Hey Barry!' though he kept his eyes on the road.

'Traffic jam!' Sam called, if any stock were being driven down the main street of Oturehua. We'd watch the mob of sheep bobbing along the road, filling the whole width of it and clattering past the cafe, sometimes into the gardens if the dogs didn't get onto them fast enough. Or there'd be cattle; brown and white beasts trotting through the village. We'd stand on the roof, hammer in hand, and watch them.

On the third day of roofing we woke to a gusting wind. We'd been blessed with the weather so far. Days and days of hot, still weather. If there'd been rain, Sam couldn't have been up on the high-pitched slopes and if there'd been gales I couldn't have rolled out the paper to fold it. Now, with all the paper creased and folded in rolls, we made the decision to keep on working and finish putting the sheets on the roof.

One roll of building paper Sam sent down to me was hurled sideways by the wind before I could catch it. I grabbed the paper and held on while it bucked and flapped in the wind. The edges began to tear. Sam struggled on the roof to hold his end down.

'It's going, let it go!' he called. And the heavy paper ripped out of my hands and ended up in a mess in the paddock. I climbed down to bring more iron over.

The wind lifted and tugged at each long-run iron sheet I staggered under. Along the road the power lines surged up and down. Even the toetoe were bent over by the wind. I pushed my gloved hands under another sheet, and hoisted it. The wind shoved me sideways.

'Are you all right?' Sam yelled.

'Yes!' I shouted back. We tried to get a last sheet of iron on to protect the paper. The iron was worse than the paper, curving and pulling at our hands, so that both of us fought to stay upright. We did get it into place, and Sam screwed it in, before calling time. The roof would have to wait.

In my old life, Dave and I had built a hut on his land in the northwest Nelson ranges. The hut was my first experience of building a house, although I didn't get to do any hammering or roofing. I sanded and primed and painted and helped mill the timber. I also kept the workers fed.

Everything was done over a fire outside: roasts cooked in a camp oven, bread and damper baked over coals, a kettle suspended from a timber frame for the never-ending cups of tea and coffee, up there on Mt Pukeone, 3000 feet above the sea. We slept in a small tent beside the fire. I bathed Evie, then a toddler, in an orange plastic tub, with water warmed up over the fire. At night we sat on logs and ate from plates on our knees. Kea circled in the dusk and called out their lonely cries. The sky filled up with stars.

When we milled the dead-standing timbers, we lugged the beams between us out of the forest on our shoulders. Evie dawdled on the track in front of us. We emerged blinking out of the forest onto the bright slopes of mountain grass. We left the world of elegant, ancient trees and mossy boulders for the world early settlers had created: the beech trees toppled and lying burnt amongst the boulders. We had to pick our way over and between the trees, their trunks blackened by fire, their textures roughened and grey as if they were driftwood tossed up on some remote shore.

And that very mountain had been a shore. Trilobites, brachiopods and shell beds help date the rocks to 60 million years ago; slopes heaved up from the ocean in some cataclysmic birthing of the land, the shoreline in one life uplifted to be ridges and folds of rock in another. Transformation on a tectonic scale.

To the Roman author Vitruvius, an engineer and architect in the first century BC, the hut was the beginning of all architecture. The simplicity of those first primitive huts, constructed from and imitating nature, is something we as humans still yearn for, says Joseph Rykwert, an architectural historian. They remind us of a time when 'man was quite at home in his house, and his houses as right as nature itself.'

Dave and I didn't know anything then about Vitruvius or the concept of the primitive hut, only that we needed to build something for shelter out of what was around us. Yet the instinct of a structure that mimicked nature – four upright trees and a canopy of branches – still led us in what we could build, from what was up there on the mountain.

Inside, the walls were bare of any lining; the floor made from planks of totara and beech. We nailed silver insulation under the floor, but in the afternoon a wind came tearing out of the west and ripped the insulation to shreds. After that, in strong gusts the mats on the floor would levitate. We held them down with chunks of firewood.

When it snowed with a wind like that, the snow forced its way through the gaps between the window frames and came in on the kitchen bench. Yet the hut was small enough to be warm if we kept the fire going throughout the day and night. Firewood lay abundantly on the hillside.

Our hut was much like the homes the pioneers first built. They too, used whatever materials were to hand, had no power, and only the need for protection. I liked to look up at the ceiling at night, at the planks and beams, and know we had milled them all, however uneven they were. And it was comforting to live in one room, with a bed and fire, and windows above the dining table that looked out on a white world. This world we were sheltered in was sufficient unto our needs.

At the old Golden Progress quartz mine, down the road from me here in Central Otago, in a narrow valley icy in winter, a notice board displays a letter from a miner who once stayed there. The miner lived in a canvas tent, and all this night he had lain with a broken arm while rain seeped into the floor. Outside, in the morning, a foot of snow chilled the air. 'The coldest most miserable night of my life,' he called it.

When we were camping by the cooking fire up on Mt Pukeone, we'd say to each other 'Won't it be great when the hut is built.' Soon we'd have a house; we could cook inside, we could sleep out of the wind. But what happened when the hut was finished and we moved in was that the wooden and iron structure separated us from living close to the land. We no longer cooked outside or sat out there to eat with the kea and the stars. We didn't lie on the ground to sleep or feel the drama of the wind. Even in that simple hut we missed the pleasure of living in the environment.

We want shelter, protection from the elements; we don't want long, miserable nights of suffering with nothing to keep us from the cold and wet. But we can be so cut off now from an awareness of where we live; what sky we have, what terrain we have, what weather we have or what plants, animals and birds live alongside us in our own place. Our *place* – that something that watches over us, participates in our moments and lasts beyond us.

The first night I stayed in my finished strawbale house, here in the Ida, I lit the fire and sat and looked around me at the walls. It was different from any house I'd ever been in. I looked at the candlelight flickering against the mud walls textured with straw. There were handprints still showing in the first coat from those who had helped to build the house.

I knew then what it was that was different. In this house the walls are made from the very material of the earth. Mud walls surround me, and as the firelight and candle flames flickered over them, creating small shadows and gleams of light, I had the distinct feeling of being inside a living, breathing structure. There was no sense of being cut off from the earth but of being held by the earth, taken care of by the earth. The house was quiet, still, warm, and has been every night since.

But long before that, before the straw went in and the roof was still open to the sky, people began to arrive for the strawbale-raising day.

My friend Bridget Auchmuty was the first, a fellow writer all the way from Nelson. I took my toolbelt off and left Sam nailing ply and went across the paddock with Bridget to help her pitch her tent. We held the flapping ends and wrestled her shelter up, then turned and watched the hills. The sun, setting low in the west, threw a golden light onto Rough Ridge, so that all the rocky tors were lit in relief. Long grass rippled away from us, golden as the tussock on the hill.

'Is that Sam yelling?' Bridget said.

We looked across to the unfinished house in the distance, and there was Sam gesturing, up on top of the roof, the sky paling behind him.

'What?' I yelled back, and started running towards him.

'The wind,' he yelled. 'It's dropping! We can finish the roof!'

PART TWO

STRAW

The walls surrounding us day in and day out need to embrace us,
our dreams and passions woven into their very fabric.
They need to sing the story of who we are.
Otherwise our houses will never become our homes.

— ATHENA AND BILL STEEN, *THE BEAUTY OF STRAW BALE HOMES*, 1994

CHAPTER 10

Mostly Older Women

Early morning in the tent, and the birds awake in the willow branches, singing up the sun. My phone rang.

'Hi Ma.'

It was daughter Merrin, up even earlier in Australia.

'Hi darling. What time is it over there?'

'Quarter to five. I'm working on a website before the girls get up. Except Scarlett's already next to me, aren't you, ratbag.'

'Tell her I've got frost on the inside of my tent.'

'Are you cold, Grandma?' That was Scarlett.

'Only when I get up.'

'It's already 23 degrees here,' Merrin said. 'The girls went swimming yesterday.'

We liked swapping temperatures, as if we lived in different hemispheres. Merrin appreciated her warm, outdoor life on the Gold Coast, though for me she was far too far away.

'Bring Ela and Lacey and Scarlett over one day when it's snowing here. I'm building a house big enough to fit you all.'

'I know, Ma. We will.'

In a weekend in March 2013, Sam and I travelled to Geraldine for another couple's bale raising. It was my first chance to have a go at cutting bales, measuring them and stacking them in a wall. There were 25 people there: Sven Johnston (who was leading the bale raising), and a group of fit men and women. Many of them had attended Sol Design's Straw Bale Design and Construction workshop. The couple's parents were also there to help with the cooking and preparing the food. It felt like such a supported venture. There were layers of experienced people and helpers, and stacks of food to keep us all going.

I saw how it worked, that a community could come together to help build a home, a passionate group of people who believed, as I did, that we could make natural houses for each other.

Over cups of tea I met some of the workers. One man, Aaron Duncan, an industrial designer, said he'd been working for 18 years on a number of working prototypes for off-grid energy generation, including a free energy machine.

'I'm not leaving this planet till I've developed some alternatives for my children,' he said. His other passion was setting up a community workshop space with tools where people could come and work on realising their ideas and inventions. He, and another man, Brent Holley, an artist, who worked educating children at schools about recycling, were adamant there had to be a paradigm shift in the way we live as a society. That we can't go on and on expecting progress and more technology and more assets at the expense of people who can't afford even the basics of food and shelter.

On the five-hour drive back that night, I told Sam it was the first time since I'd had the dream as a teenager of people building a house together that I had actually seen it in action. Up till then it had been just an idea I'd believed in, something I'd read about. Now I'd taken part in a bale-raising day; I'd been one of many who had come together, not for money but for learning, to help someone else reach their dream.

In the Ida Valley, two major obstacles were keeping me awake at night. The first was that I couldn't get a strawbale expert to come on the day of the bale raising. Sam had taken a ten-day course in strawbale building in Geraldine, but Sven Johnston, who taught the course, was busy on a bale project closer up his way. He gave me the names of other experienced people but they were also too busy.

One man did say he would come to the site the week before the bale day and go over everything with us. He'd make sure we were confident in what we were doing with the bales. I was relieved because I wasn't feeling confident at all. But now it was Thursday, two days before bale day, and the man still hadn't come.

The second obstacle was not having enough people to come to my bale raising. Geraldine was a centre of strawbale building and many people there were locals and could get easily to the site to help. My project was down in the depths of Central Otago. I was new to the area and didn't have many contacts. My old friends lived 12 hours away by car. Though the message had gone out through any strawbale-building channels we knew of, people couldn't travel or the date didn't suit for those who were keen.

I went through the people who had promised to come: there was Sam and I, pregnant Hana, writer Bridget and Sam's mum, Julie, both in their sixties. Brian would be there, making it three writers, and hopefully Declan, the magician and film-maker. My son Nick would be on standby at the airport to get a flight from Auckland, making him, apart from Hana and Sam, the only person under 54 years of age on the site.

Sam put a message up on Facebook to all his friends, and the only one who said they could come was a friend's mother, Bridget Henry, a woman of my age. She lived over in the next valley, and she promised she would be there. And I had an email from someone called Pat Shuker in Twizel, who was keen to come. Was Pat a man or woman? Older or younger than the rest of us? Because we were sorely short of manpower.

I'd seen the men at last week's bale-raising gleefully using the sledgehammer to pound walls into shape. They swung from the rafters while they literally booted a bale tightly in, taking turns to outdo themselves with strength and laughing like it was boys' own fun.

Bridget A. had had a double hip replacement, I had a sore back and Brian more broken bones and injuries than he cared to remember. I knew we wouldn't be doing such vigorous work.

'How are you going securing people for the bale day?' Philippa asked when she brought the coffee over to our table at the cafe.

'It seems to be mostly older people or women. Mostly older women,' I said. 'And none of us knows what we're doing.'

'Well, Mum and I will come over and help when the cafe closes,' she said.

'I'm so grateful to you,' I said. 'I know how busy you are, too. We'll all just do it, somehow!'

When I went up to pay, a man with a big smile came over to me at the counter. 'I heard about your strawbale house,' he said. 'I'll be there on Saturday. I wouldn't miss it for anything.' We shook hands. This was Graeme Male. He was busy helping build his own house down the road, an import like me, though he was from Auckland. He shared the same passion for community.

That night as Sam and I were packing the tools up in the near dark on the building site, Philippa came over from the cafe with a plate of muffins for us.

'We wish we could be there to help all Saturday,' she said. 'But we'll be there when we can.'

The next morning, Sam and I looked down from the roof to see his father Dennis's truck pull in. Dennis is a Harley Davidson motorcyclist, an artist, and a great do-it-yourselfer; he once built a five-storey house, designed by Wellington

Roof on, all ready for the bales.

architect Ian Athfield, on his own, with help from Sam's mum, Julie.

Dennis, Bridget and I began the task of loading straw from the Becks' hay-shed down the road and bringing it up to the site. Bridget worked hard, clamber-ing over the unstable bales to help me on the stack, and Dennis stood on his truck and lifted them up in high layers.

He'd had a serious heart attack a few years ago, flat-lining twice before they could bring him back. He had pills now, he said, to keep him going. He stopped now and again to wipe the sweat from his face and take a breather from loading. On the first trip back to the site, the bales six high and also stacked on top of the driver's cab, Dennis told Bridget and me of all the times he'd nearly died, or died and come back from the void: once by drowning, once by electrical shock, once by car accident, twice by heart attack.

'You just have to live the life you're happy with,' he said. 'That's what I've learnt. That's why I love taking people on motorbike tours across America. They're out on the bikes and we're heading from New York to Chicago, they're not thinking about their bills or mortgages or work. They love it. People don't want to go home again.'

We took three more loads of straw before I said we'd better leave it at that for the day. I wondered again how Brian and I had heaved the whole truckload of bales that other morning.

That night Sam, Bridget, Dennis and I went down to the pub for a meal and the traditional round of drinks to celebrate a roof going on; the roof shout. The pub was quiet, only two men at the bar, both workers from Beckers. A shy smile from Col Leishman, who would patiently find me tool parts or take care of welding jobs for me when I went down to their shed, and a big grin from Grim Corfield, who often drove the truck bringing us timber or gravel or anything else we needed, sometimes at ten minutes' notice.

'What will you drink?' I asked them. I bought Graeme, the publican, a drink as well, one for his wife Liz who was out the back cooking the meals, and one for a young man who came in to use his laptop.

A few days later a farmer said to me, 'I see you've got the roof on. When's the roof shout?'

'We've already had it,' I said. 'I shouted the whole pub.'

CHAPTER 11

You're Such an Egg

The wind shrieked all day, all night, flexed
whatever muscles it wanted,

flattened the new peas, bowled the outdoor toilet,
the neighbour's chicken coop flew over

the fence (the hens were spared).
The restless air stopped flights, closed

roads, upended my shed
in a tree. A starling,

grass in beak, blew
backwards past the window ...

–excerpt from 'Wind in the Ida' by Jillian Sullivan

Anything that could move during the building process would take off in those Ida Valley gale winds. We lost tarpaulins to the fence lines by the road and one tarpaulin I'd rigged over the caravan hardly lasted a week. To protect the new interior walls of the house, Sam had long lengths of 4×2 nailed up diagonally as bracing all through the framework.

To go anywhere on site meant ducking. Every room entrance had the slash of timber across it. It was either climb under or over whenever I had to get tools or get from one job to another. Hitting my head became one of those hazards on the job that, try as I could, I couldn't avoid. One day, after lifting heavy beams for hours and the incessant nailing of bracing, I said to Sam, 'That was a hard day and I'm glad it's over.' I then turned around and walked straight into the timber again.

'You have to make a decision not to do that anymore,' Sam said. 'In the first year of my apprenticeship I hit my head on site all the time. I made a decision I was not going to. You have to decide that, and totally commit to it and believe it. I haven't hit my head again.'

'I have said that to myself,' I said. 'And it doesn't work.'

'You have to say it and believe it. And stay aware the whole time.'

Commitment to safety and awareness.

On one job Sam had been on, the contractor called the men together, Sam and two other builders, and told them, 'You guys be careful up there. I don't want any of you falling off that roof.'

'It was a tricky roof, too,' Sam said. 'Two storeys high, a strong wind, and we had to walk carrying the sheets of iron, stepping across the rafters. We had to really decide we were going to be safe that day.'

I added that to my list of what builders had to be – acrobats; people aware of their bodies every moment.

Sam always dressed well on site. He wore good jeans and Merino tops and a greenstone pendant each day to work. Reflecting back now I see he brought his professionalism to the job in every aspect. He made sure we left the site tidy each night for a clean start in the morning; he kept his tools in his work van in boxes he'd constructed to protect them. And he looked smart.

I thought being on a work site meant you wore whatever you could find. I wore grey and white camo shorts passed down to me from Sam's mum. I liked them for how I could roll them up in the heat, then roll them down again when my legs started to burn. I wore an old red tartan shirt that once belonged to the elderly man I looked after as a nurse aid in the weekends. I had my hair in plaits, old work boots I got from an op shop for two dollars, and my daughter's Australian digger's hat. Perhaps the way I dressed reflected my inexperienced attitude to building.

If Sam wasn't happy about the way a particular section of building had gone, he'd do it over again.

'But that will be fine as it is,' I'd say.

'Not on any house I build,' Sam would reply, and on a rare error he made, he stayed behind on his own time to fix it.

I know when it comes to writing, I attempt that same care and thoughtfulness, and can relate to that quote of Gustave Flaubert's: 'I spent the morning putting in a comma and the afternoon removing it.'

As for my building outfit, it worked for me. But one morning, loading tools into the work van from the shed by the caravan, Sam said to me, 'You look like one of those extras on the *Hobbit* films.'

'What do you mean?' I was shocked. 'I think I look pretty good.' He laughed, and we posed for a photo together to record our outfits before heading up to the site. That morning he finally put in a stile for climbing the fence to go to the cafe. We'd given up going once a week and now just accepted we went for a coffee to the 'office' every day. I'd go ahead of Sam to order while he kept working till the last minute, then I'd yell 'Coffee!' across the paddock when it was ready. This morning, as I climbed over the new stile for the first time, he called out,

'Hey, you've got style!'

Really? I smiled to myself. I'd swapped my camo shorts for my ripped Levis, and I thought Sam must have changed his mind about the *Hobbit* comment.

When Philippa passed me the coffees, she said, 'I hear you've got stile,' and I thought, wow, she thinks so too, then realised, oh, it was a pun all along. I was back to being a hobbit.

I told Sam I'd misunderstood him about the style/stile and he said, 'You're such an egg.'

We'd taken that phrase from the New Zealand movie *Boy* and looked for any chance on site to say it to each other. I was an egg so much Sam said he needed to have one carved for me.

The classic episode was when we trucked in all the roofing materials and gutters and flashings and laid them out in the paddock. I was proud of all the shiny red materials that would soon be my roof. It started to rain then, big heavy drops. The gutters were face up to the sky, and I said to Sam, 'Do you think they'll be all right out here in the rain?'

He just looked at me. 'That's what gutters are for, you egg.'

I caught Sam out a good one, though, when he finally got to use the new staple gun we'd ordered. We needed it to speed up nailing wire netting along the beams for the mud plastering. I tried to pass Sam the instruction sheet.

'I don't need instructions,' he said.

On the second day the staple gun started to smoke. That was it, it was wrecked. He tried taking it to pieces, and finally read the instructions on the box. 'Fill with oil before each use.'

'You're such an egg,' I said.

Baling needles, my American 'how-to' strawbale book said, were required to re-sew the straw bales. We would have to cut many of the bales to fit in the walls, which meant pushing a needle through them and retying the bales with baling twine. We would also need to sew the bales to the window frames to ensure the walls kept straight until the mud plaster went on. There was no picture of a baling needle in the book and no description of how to use one, only an address in California where you could buy them. That didn't help out in Oturehua.

My first sight of a bale needle was when we went to the bale-raising day in Geraldine. Oh, so that was what they were. Not needles with an eye at all, but long pieces of steel with a handle at the top for bracing your weight to push them through the bales, and slots filed on the end.

The needles had one slot in one direction to hook the baling twine and push it through the bale, and one filed the other direction for hooking the twine and pulling it back through the bale. That way you could sew bales together or sew bales to the posts and to the window frames.

The best baling needles we saw in Geraldine were made of slim shiny steel, easy for pushing through the bales. We didn't have any of these on site, and true to our ethos of using whatever we had to hand, we decided on using the leftover rebar steel rods, the long rods with a twisted texture down their sides that we'd used in the concrete pad.

Sam drew a design on an offcut of macrocarpa and I took it down to trusty Beckers with the rods. Col welded small offcuts of rebar on to the top of each half-metre-long rod to be our handles. Back on site Dennis used a grinder to polish smooth the last few inches of the rods and file the slots into the ends.

The browned-off grass was crunchy under our feet and the air temperature about 35 degrees. Dennis was out in the glare of the sun, away from any building materials and the stack of precious straw. Periodically I hosed the ground around him to stop any sparks from igniting.

The baling needles ended up looking like medieval weapons. They looked so handsome Sam said he would mount them, crossed, like a coat of arms, on the rectangle of wall we left unplastered as the 'truth' window in one of the sitting-room walls.

The truth window is a tradition of strawbale building. A piece of wall is left with glass over the straw to show the structure of the house beneath its covering of mud. Bare straw – the truth of the building.

As far as baling needles go, however, rebar would have to be one of the most difficult materials to have chosen. Every time you pushed the needle into the straw it was a fight of tensions between the tightly compressed roughage of the

Dennis with a finished baling needle.

bale and the textured steel. Four needles costing about fifteen dollars each for smooth steel would have been a much better investment of our time and effort.

As owner-builder of my strawbale house, I enjoy the challenge of recycling, making do and being inventive, rather than paying for something ready made. Another example of this making do was with the moisture meters. These are required by the council for every strawbale building, as they give advance warning of any developing dampness. They're placed under all windowsills and doorways, places where rain could get in. Basically, they're an inert material with wooden blocks attached, each of which has wires running from them and then the wires are fed back to a central board and labelled. A moisture meter reader is then placed on the terminal points of each meter and will read if there is any

81

moisture getting into the block of wood placed at the sill under the bales.

I knew throughout the whole project I had to make moisture meters, 24 of them. I thought I would gradually make them at nights, after the working day. I thought they would be easy enough. Yet every night I was so physically worn out; too tired to hardly cook dinner, too tired to eat, too tired to think. I put off making the meters and forgot about them. Until the night before Bridget arrived, two days before the bale-raising day, and Sam said, 'We've forgotten the moisture meters!'

The house simply could not continue until the meters were in place. The bales would be so tightly compressed in the walls it would be impossible to put them in then. And I couldn't get the house signed off by council with a code of compliance unless the moisture meters were there.

'That's all right. Bridget and I will make them tomorrow,' I said.

I needed plastic for the inert material. Something like a big white bucket. I sifted through the site and down by the shed, but nothing. Brian went through his shed and garden and found a bucket a friend had given him planted with potatoes. Brian tipped the old soil out, I scrubbed the bucket and Sam cut it into 24 long strips with the skill saw.

For the wooden blocks, Sam took offcuts of macrocarpa and used the drop saw to make 72 small squares, three each for the meters. Bridget and I drilled screw holes in the blocks then screwed them into the white plastic strips.

Stripping the telephone wire and attaching it under the screws was no fun. First, we didn't have the right tools, only knives that kept cutting the wires right through, which meant starting again. It was a long, fiddly job for people who had never done that sort of work before. I had to leave Bridget to do it as my task was to run the rest of the moisture meter wires through the entire house.

'Climb up the framing here,' Sam said. 'You can weave the wires under this beam, find some way to get them through this top beam, you'll have to get my drill out the back of the van and drill holes through here and here, and for that top window, bring the wires up through this point, run them along here, and ...'

My eyes glazed over. I couldn't cope with long strings of instructions. I remembered I had to drill holes but I couldn't remember the size drill bit Sam said and I knew enough not to re-ask him when he was busy. I was better at being given instructions for one thing, doing it, then being told what to do next.

I stood and looked up the wall frame and along the beam where I was supposed to thread wires. Bridget was doing her best to cope, sitting in the corner with the plastic on her knees and fumbling with the wires. Sam was up in the roof space swinging his nail gun as if it weighed nothing, racing against time to put plywood sheets as stops for the bales we'd place in the morning. I wasn't an electrician and I'd never run wires. How was I going to do all the work that needed to be done by the morning? I started to run out the cable, tacking it as I went with fiddly cable ties.

After a while I started to get a feel for the task. It was a clean job; white cable along sweet-smelling macrocarpa beams. Not dangerous, just awkward, getting in and out of tight spaces, but anything that wasn't dangerous was good. No heights.

By mid-afternoon Bridget had completed five moisture meters. I'd run out only half the cable. We had to stop what we were both doing to shift more truckloads of straw. By dusk we were all exhausted. The idea that we would sit up late by torch and lamplight struggling with the meters became unrealistic.

And the strawbale expert had not turned up. All day I'd still believed he would come. Wasn't the mentor supposed to arrive when you committed to the journey? Weren't Sam and I as committed as could be?

I thought of how Sven had made the speech to all the volunteers at the bale raising in Geraldine. It had felt safe to have an expert encouraging people, teaching them what to do, checking up on them all day that the bales were going in correctly. I needed someone to check up on me. I wasn't the right person to be teaching others or checking up on them. Everyone who was coming was a novice at baling walls.

It had been hard enough doing the food list – sitting late at night in my tent two nights earlier, trying to figure out a menu for lunch and dinner and texting Sam's mum a long list of supplies for her to bring from the supermarket when she drove down from Christchurch. Now she was here, and the food stacked in boxes in her car to protect from mice, and chilled enough in the cold nights here without a fridge.

Sam and I made a decision that we wouldn't work on into the night on the meters. We were all tired, and tomorrow would start at 7 a.m. That would give us three hours before the scheduled start time for the bale raising.

I helped Sam lift the drop saw into the back of the van and unbuckled my toolbelt. Whatever the next day would bring, we had done all we could for tonight.

CHAPTER 12

We'll Figure it Out

Usually Friday night was the end of our working week. Up until the two weeks before the bale-raising day, we'd pack up at 5 p.m., then Sam would head home to his family, and I'd drive 130 km to my weekend job. I'd catch sight of the Hawkduns turning pink in the sunset in my rear-vision mirror, and feel a pang of separation. On Black's Hill, near Ophir, I'd stop, if I had time, and look across the Ida Valley and its boundary of blue-ridged mountains. In a few days I'd be back again, but for six months, each weekend in Arrowtown, I helped look after a gracious 87-year-old man named Jim.

'I'm going to dance at your wedding,' Jim had said to me the last time I'd seen him. I'd reached across and put my hand on his.

'Thank you, Jim. I would love that.' We were sat on a stone wall looking across a pond. I was pressed close to him so he'd stay upright. There wasn't a wedding in sight for me, and Jim wouldn't be dancing. But I think if there was a wedding, and he could dance, of course he would be there.

'Let's go home now, Jim.' I helped him up. It was Saturday morning and I'd been looking out for him since seven the night before. We turned and looked back the way we'd come: along the pond, past the lupins in flower and the neighbour's vegetable garden planted in brassicas.

'That's not my house,' Jim said, when I pointed out the cottage. 'It's this way.' He looked up towards a pinetree-lined road. I knew he wouldn't make it, walking that far, the long way home. And every house we passed that way wouldn't be his house, whether he thought it was or not.

What shape is the home he believes is his? What home does he live in in his heart? Maybe it's his last home, from which he walked to work each day, returned home again for lunch, and still returns to now in his mind.

I ignored the cottage beyond the pond, its verandah with clematis and new bulbs, and pointed out a duck to Jim. He leant against his cane and we watched the small brown mallard fluff her wings and settle on the water near the reeds.

'Do you think there are ducklings, Jim? They might be this way.'

We did see two half-grown ducks in the sun between lupin plants. After that there was a flowering cherry tree for us to examine. In this way we made it back to his verandah.

'This looks a nice place,' he said. 'Should we knock?'

The door was already open.

'No, let's go inside,' I said. 'It's your home, Jim. This is where you live.'

I wonder sometimes, when our bodies move from one home to another, if our souls want to keep believing there is just one home. They take some convincing to shift. Not long after my husband and I had broken up (broken being an appropriate verb for this situation) I came down with the flu. I lay on my bed in a rented house and it struck my fevered mind that I should get up, walk out the door, and go back to my real home and my life where we were all together.

That home was gone, sold, my gum trees and my vegetable garden someone else's. *But you can still go back*, my mind told me, *you can just walk in.* I thought, after that breakup, that when I died I would go back to my gum-tree farm and look at every plant I'd planted and lean my forehead against the wooden planked side of the house one last time.

There have been four houses since then, including the hut up in the mountains. I'd have a bit of travelling and saying goodbye to do, every home imbued with some of my life. I think of how buildings shelter us and comfort us, and gardens, too, especially those sprung from gifted cuttings and seeds and seedling trees.

Yet I cannot imagine a life that didn't have *this* home in it.

On the building site, this Friday night, the tools were stacked in the van and the house peaceful under the new moon rising. I looked at the dark, tarpaulined stack of straw bales waiting for the morning. The raising day almost upon us, and still no one to teach us.

How would that stack turn into my house? Right up till the sun set I believed the man would turn up to advise us. All these people coming, all this work to do. At that moment, in the near dark, I felt overwhelmed with responsibility.

'What about the expert?' I said again to Sam.

Bridget and Julie had gone down to the caravan to make dinner. Dennis had gone back to Queenstown and would return next week. Sam lifted the drop saw into the back of the van and swung the door shut.

'We haven't got enough men for the heavy work,' I said, 'and we haven't got anyone to show us what to do.'

'Look at this structure,' said Sam. 'Who built this house?'

I looked across at the frames of the house under its new roof.

'You and me.'

'Well, we're going to kick it at the strawbale day. Anyone else who turns up is a bonus. It's only walls with straw in it. We'll figure it out.'

I remembered then that sometimes the mentor that arises is your own self; the strengths you have within you, your own courage, your own skills and intuition and readiness to work – these become the mentor energy.

Sam said we could do it, and so I took heart from that.

It was too late now to change anything anyway. The meters weren't ready. The wires weren't all run. Sam hadn't finished putting up the bale stops. Yet Hana and the grandchildren were coming in the morning. And Nick had texted to say he'd paid for his flight to make sure he would be here too. Julie was here and though not able to work because of arthritis, she would take care of the food. Graeme from down the road had said he would come. Brian had had to go to Dunedin but he would be here when he could. Declan might be able to make it. Bridget from the next valley would definitely come.

And like Sam said, everyone that came was a bonus to the two of us, and we would just work it out.

We drove down to the shed, unloaded the drop saw and the boxed tools and went into the warmth and light of the caravan. We squeezed up to eat Thai tofu curry by candlelight: Sam, his mum, Bridget and I; a builder and three women near retirement age, and the day of straw in the morning.

Julie went out to the car to get plums for dessert.

'There are car lights down at the house,' she said.

I took a torch and went out into the dark. Sure enough, there was a vehicle parked on the house site, a white farm ute. As I got closer a small terrier jumped down from the ute, then someone with strong legs, in shorts, a big red bushshirt, and with tousled dark grey hair.

'Gidday,' she said. 'I'm Pat.'

'Hi. I'm Jillian. You're just in time for dinner.'

Pat squeezed in as well on the bed in the caravan, and Julie passed her a bowl of rice and curry.

'You've had a big drive,' I said. 'Thank you so much for coming.'

Pat had driven four-and-a-half hours to a building site, to complete strangers.

And like the workers the house was attracting, she was a woman, an older woman like the rest of us.

'What do you do, Pat?' Sam asked.

'Do? I don't do anything,' she said. 'I'm seventy-three.'

'Have you built a strawbale house before?' I asked her.

'I've helped build them all round the world,' said Pat. 'I thought I'd come and help you build yours.'

Our mentor had arrived.

CHAPTER 13
The Team

All week rain had been forecast for Saturday. Weather was the one thing we could not do anything about. But Saturday dawned calm and cloudless, cold but fine. Pat had insisted on sleeping outdoors, and Sam had made a bed for her on some straw bales under the stars.

'I can sleep anywhere,' she said. 'I've got a sleeping bag that goes to 50 degrees below.'

She was up and about taking care of her little dog when we arrived on site at seven. I told her about the moisture meters, how much we needed them and how far behind we were on schedule.

'That's all right,' said Pat. 'I'll learn to make them and then I'll sit here, all day if necessary, until they're finished.' Bridget shared her hard-won knowledge with Pat. They sat together on the window framing, bent over their knives and wires.

The other Bridget arrived early from the next valley and she and Julie took on the job of bucketing the small stones Grim had delivered and tipping them into the channel between the double floor plate of 4×2s. Later in the day the first straw bales would sit on top of that floor plate. The gravel, on a blanket of black polythene siliconed to the floor plates, would take any moisture in the bales into the depth of stones and give it a chance to evaporate.

I was up in the frames running wires; on the stereo Julia and Angus Stone played. I looked at the four older women bent to their tasks: two complete strangers, a woman who had come into my family by marriage and my own dear friend. They had travelled from Nelson, from Christchurch, from Twizel and from the next valley to help raise up a home. They brought, if not experience or skills, then willingness to do what it took to get a job done, patience to sit with something until the fingers learnt how to do it, strength in sore bones to keep lifting a bucket.

We had no idea how we would make the straw walls rise up. We didn't know how

Moisture meters in place above the gravel.

long it would take or if everything would turn out well. Pat, when she'd been on crutches from a truck crash at work in England, had lost her job as a horse trainer. With nowhere to live and no money, she'd camped, injured, in her car to protest outside her former employer's gates.

Writer Bridget had left behind an alcoholic husband and shifted across the world to make a new start without memories. Now her loved partner of 18 years was dead. Newly widowed, she had been scared to come away from her home, to come to a place she didn't know amongst people she didn't know, unsure of her skills. Yet she had come.

Julie's friend's sister was dying of a sudden and fast cancer. Julie wanted to be here with her son and grandchildren, treasuring the time to be with the people she loves.

Bridget Henry's daughter was in labour in hospital at the other end of the country. Bridget couldn't be there with her daughter, and so she came to us, to offer her own strength for the walls of my house, while she waited for a baby to be safely born.

In stories from South America, recalled in *Women Who Run With the Wolves* by Clarissa Pinkola Estés, there's an ancient crone, known by some as La Loba, who is said to be inside each of us. La Loba hunts in the darkness, in the mountains, in the dry river beds, for the fragments of bones of once-dead wolves. She gathers them together, she assembles the white skeleton of what was, and then by the fire she thinks about the song she will sing.

The song rises up in her, not by thought now, but by the essence of the bones in front of her, of the silent song of their own bone sculpture. La Loba sings their song back to them, and the bones begin to grow flesh. The flesh grows wolf pelt, the tail rises, exuberant and full. The ancient one sings from a place deep within her own bones, until the creature, fully formed, leaps up and runs out into the wilderness. And there, under moonlight or sunlight or from a river's wild blessing, the wolf turns into a woman laughing.

How it is that we sing each other's lives back into fullness. How we help each other travel that road to who we were.

At ten in the morning, Hana arrived from Queenstown with Indy and Phoenix, and Nick, from Auckland, who sat straight down to help finish the moisture meters. The new neighbour Graeme Male arrived, bringing his own tools and the experience of another life he'd led as a chippie for seven years. He lived here now, setting up a bed and breakfast with his wife, Donna, an international air hostess, in this place he'd fallen in love with one day as he'd passed through on a bike.

'When I biked through Poolburn Viaduct towards Thurlow Road and saw the Ida Valley for the first time, spread out under that wide blue sky, I felt it almost like a blow within my body,' he'd told me. 'It was a vision so insistent, I thought, when I die I'd like to come back in another life here. Then one day, back in Auckland, I thought, why don't I go in this lifetime?' At age 60 he gave up his job to shift from one end of New Zealand to the other, for no other reason than the mountains called to him.

He brought his wide grin to strawbale-raising day and to the days that came after, through straw compressing and mud plastering, and his cheerful attitude buoyed us. Sam and I took to calling Graeme 'Mr Motivator', and invariably at the end of a long day, when Sam and I felt we couldn't do any more, Graeme would

The morning baling team: Graeme, Julie, Declan, Indy, Nick, Phoenix, Hana, Bridget A., Bridget Henry, Sam and Pat.

turn up from his own project, pull on his ever-present gloves and help us for a while.

It was he who first called us all The Team, one day when we were converging at the cafe. Graeme went down at ten each day, and Sam and I were there not long after. I'd text Brian and he'd leave his computer in his book-lined office and join us and whoever else was on the site that day. Our long discussions always included the environment, and how were we to protect the land we have rights to, yet have responsibilities to as well. These responsibilities travel beyond society's own version of progress to include the wellbeing of all of us: birds, animals, fish, rivers, trees, air and mountains. Or as Brian likes to quote from Aldo Leopold: the world around us is 'a community to which we belong' rather than 'a commodity belonging to us'.

By lunchtime, with Bridget, Pat and Nick on the arduous task, the moisture meters were all in place. I'd run the wires, Graeme and Sam had finished the bale stops in the ceiling, and Declan, with dog Grover, had arrived from Dunedin. We sat on the bales and Sam and Pat stood out the front with a bale and a bale needle and a length of twine.

Now, at last, with a real teacher in Pat, we had the opening speech and the instructions on how to proceed.

CHAPTER 14

A Strawbale Raising

The strawbale building movement is about 160 years old. It was begun in America after the first baling machines arrived in 1850. Of course, people have built with straw and clay for thousands of years, as long as they've built houses. There are straw homes in Germany 500 years old and still lived in. But the use of compressed bales for a house is a recent advent.

In New Zealand, bale houses have only been built since the 1970s. As each house has mostly been owner built, although there are specific strawbale building companies now, techniques have been evolving. Each house is a one-off, and has its own quirks and challenges. Builders and co-builders come up with their own innovations – as Sam and Nick did for me with their improvisations.

That's part of the fun of building with straw. No one knows the answer to everything. There's not one right way of doing something. As long as you start out with dry straw and compress it, you are free to work out the best way to do that.

When an architect draws a plan, they suppose that timber will be the length and width it says it is, and be so uniformly. When a farmer bales straw, the bales come out the baler in approximate lengths and weights. Bales are not the same size. I didn't know this, nor how much extra work this would entail. A layer in a wall doesn't take exactly 5 bales, but 4.7 bales, or 5.2 bales, depending on the size of each original bale. Hence, the uses to which bale needles have to be put.

The main difficulty with resizing and retying bales in order to get them fitting correctly into the length of wall, is how hard it is to compress the bales back to the pressure they were under when done by machine. The way we had been shown to tighten the strings in Geraldine was to lean over the bale and use our weight to compress the sheaves of straw while retying the string. This worked well enough for tall people, mostly the men, but for me it meant I lay across the top of a bale with my feet off the ground as if I was about to nose dive into the concrete, launched by a bale of straw.

93

Nick explains his new method for resizing and retying bales to Pat and Hana, while the bales go into the walls behind them.

Nick came up with a new method. He was once a sailor, spending five years sailing the world on super yachts before going back to university to be an engineer, and he knows his knots. It would be a lot quicker, he said, if we used two loops for purchase, as if we had two pulleys made of rope. The mechanical advantage of the two loops meant that the twine could be pulled as tight as a guitar string – without lifting our feet off the ground.

Pat, the Bridgets and I used this method without tipping over, and although it was hard on our hands, gloves helped. So did a further tweaking of the method: using the claw of a hammer, threading the twine between the hammer claws, and twisting the hammer to tighten the twine. Soon we were all measuring bales like professionals, cutting twine, making knots, tightening bales, and stacking them in a brickwork pattern in the first wall.

Inside the house, we each took a segment of wall, beginning with the long back wall. We came to grips with getting our bales in place, eventually layering them up five bales high, ready for compressing. Here Sam and I would roll out our new technique with custom-made steel plates, which Sam had designed and Beckers had made up for us. Steel plates and truck strops, this was Sam's answer to the dilemma of how to compress a wall of straw.

We didn't have a way of testing out our steel-plate method before the raising day, what with needing bales up in the wall first. Now, with everyone gathered round to watch, Sam lifted the large steel plate up onto the top bale of straw in a new wall of bales. The aim was to compress the wall down firmly using truck strops so there was room to slide the last bale in under the ceiling. We would then release the pressure on the wall, the bales would spring back up and lock into a tight wall.

Sam passed the truck strops over the bale, hooked them on the narrow steel plates bolted to the floor plates and Graeme and Declan began to ratchet the strops down, Graeme outside on the right-hand strop, Declan inside on the left-hand strop.

'The wall needs to come down evenly so it doesn't twist,' Sam said. 'Graeme, you go now; ok, now you, Declan.' The strops clicked and creaked as they tightened.

'The bale's moving down,' I said. 'I can see it!'

Sam held his tape measure to the gap.

'390 mm,' he said. 'Keep it coming. Declan, more on your side.'

The men took turns racheting, and bit by bit the bales compressed. For the last effort Graeme leaned in towards the wall, hauling up with all his strength.

'That's it,' said Sam. 'Good job!' He lifted the last bale and pushed it in on top. The steel plate slid out easily, the strops came off, and the wall locked into place.

'You beauty!' said Graeme. '*Go* the strawbale house!' I grinned back at him and Sam. My bedroom wall was no longer a framework of timber but a textured, golden mass. Graeme gathered the strops up and I bent with the drill to unscrew the steel from the floor plate. Sam crouched beside me, his drill in hand, ready to move the steel for the next section.

'You did it, Sam,' I said. We nodded at each other.

'Now we can keep going,' he said.

I took a deep breath of the fragrance of straw. Straightened up. Across from me Hana sat on a straw bale, measuring and cutting twine. Phoenix and Indy squatted over offcuts of wood in the dust at her feet. At the corner of the house, Bridget A. leant into her bale, pushing it into position.

'I need a bale at least 960 long for the top here,' said Sam.

'I've got one,' said Nick.

I picked up the weight of my own bale and carried it towards the house.

One factor we hadn't taken into consideration was how long it takes to chainsaw a section out of bales for them to fit snugly round the posts. Other strawbale houses, using a different design, place the bales up on their narrow edge instead of flat like my plan. These houses incorporate the structural posts between the bales, which means almost no time spent chainsawing the bales to fit and more time spent on stacking bales. That is, faster installation.

My walls had numerous posts to fit around. The chainsawing became the place where we got held up. Another week into the project the chainsaw blew up and a replacement had to be found. That also suffered being clogged with straw, and a third chainsaw finished the job. We learnt the hard way that an electric chainsaw is much the easier way to go, not so loud, no fumes, lighter to handle. Some builders use a small circular blade and swear by that, but Sam thought they looked dangerous.

An even better way to go is start with a design that cuts out the need for repeated chainsawing of the bales to fit round the posts. We didn't know enough of the variety of structural systems at the beginning of the project to even know what we didn't know. We just had to live with the slow progress.

In my imagination, weeks before the bale-raising day, when I wasn't scaremongering myself in the middle of the night with visions of no one coming or the walls falling over, I pictured the bales all going in on the one day, the walls finished and my house nearly done.

In reality, we got the back wall in and part way up two sides. My bedroom almost had two outside walls. I could see the window shaped by straw. We had a long way to go to get the house finished, especially if it was mainly Sam and me to do it.

But that was the future. For now, I worked from bale to bale – measuring, retying, carrying the bales over to layer them in their exact place in the wall. And all the while I felt as if I were floating. I was *in* my dream, and not alone but on a site busy with people working alongside me.

For 25 years I had envisioned the possibility of people coming together to build a natural, sustainable house. I had believed in community. And here we were helping Sam: son, daughter, grandchildren, in-laws, neighbours, friends and new friends, none of us a builder, building a house.

Bridget A. uses a good kick to give sideways compression in the wall.

The rain that had threatened all week began to look a reality: a big arch of grey sky overhead and the Hawkduns and Mt Ida a steely blue under the darkening sky. There were 200 bales stacked outside. It was nearly five o'clock when we began the task of carrying the bales into the house. Brian was back from Dunedin in time to help. The cafe shut a little earlier and Philippa and Barbara came over with their wheelbarrow. Instead of bale walls, the house grew interior golden structures. And when we had finished and the straw was safe, the rain pelted down.

We stood together under the eaves of the house to share a meal. We drank champagne. I toasted everyone and thanked each one for what they'd done that day, and for their gifts of time and steadfastness. I said it was, apart from births and marriage, the happiest day of my life. Then Graeme raised his glass and made a toast.

'Here's to having a dream and to following it,' he said.

That night I slept in the house for the first time, a duvet and pillow on a bed made of straw bales. My bale bed was where the bathroom would be. Pat had a straw bed in my bedroom, and Nick made his up on the stack in the front of the house, seven bales high, just because he could. I wriggled on the hard surface of the bale in an attempt at comfort. That princess and the pea story, that's how I felt.

The rain drummed heavier on the roof, yet we were all dry, and every bale of straw too. I could feel the chill of wind on my cheeks and pulled the duvet close. Nick and Pat were already asleep. It was a comfort to know they were there, sharing the first night. I lay there going over images of the day. Everything had changed. The tarpaulined pile of straw on the grass was now stacked in the building, and in the walls. The house dark and quiet and smelling of dry grass. Almost a home, sheltering us.

Outside, Declan slept in his van, Julie in her car, Bridget in her tent, and Hana, Sam and the kids in the caravan. In the morning we would all come together and begin again.

When the girls were little, I learnt what it's like to live in cold, substandard housing. Suffice it to say, it's hard on your body and it's hard on your mind. I felt an outsider in my own community. I don't believe the solution to housing is to increase the number of houses we build by methods we already use. 'Stick houses' Sam calls them now; houses made of thin lengths of timber and gypsum, coated in an array of expensive, toxic materials, and a constant challenge to keep heat inside in winter.

There needs to be a shift in the kind of housing we build. Shelter is our right. No less than the animals and birds, we have the right to a home, and we shouldn't have to have a lifelong mortgage to do so. In 2013 I wrote to the Children's Commissioner, pointing out that as a society in the Western world, we've forgotten we are capable of providing our own housing. I said, 'Housing has become the right only of those who can afford it. I believe the solution is for communities to build houses, and to build them out of natural, sustainable, cheap resources; houses healthy and warm to live in.'

Bring on the straw, the mud and the grandmothers, I say.

The morning after the bale raising we emerged from our various cocoons and resumed work together. We ended with a lunch, the last of the food spread out on the work trestle, and Declan performed magic for us.

Graeme gets ready to ratchet.

Declan had once performed magic in Hollywood, at glittering balls in Hong Kong, and in movies and advertisements. Now, especially for Indy and Phoenix, and the rest of the grown kids around the table, he pulled coins from the air in my straw-stacked house, made plums appear and disappear in front of the children's faces, and though we stared and stared we couldn't see how he did it.

'A little trick I learnt,' he said, as he tumbled coins right through the table, 'from a magician named Tony Slydini. He built a beautiful routine around this trick and made his living from it. Tony learnt the move from a student of the great Canadian magician Dai Vernon, aka The Professor. And Dai Vernon learnt the move from a travelling Chinese magician, Han Ping Chien. So there you have it.' He lifted the silver coins from below the table to show us. 'The magic has come full circle.'

Inherent in the substance of straw is the ability for it to decompose, to combust, to heat up to high temperatures, to break down into glucose and sugary stalks. A strawbale house has to be kept dry at all times, from harvest time through to construction. Once it has become soaked, even though a bale dries out, the process of decomposition has already begun within it.

A few months later, on the Becks' farm where I still had a hundred bales of straw stored, the shed crumpled in high winds and exposed the bales to rain. I was away, and Declan and Pat raced to save the leftover straw, which was going to its new home in Twizel for Pat's building.

Kept dry, the straw in strawbale walls lasts the lifetime of the building, and will outlast us for hundreds of years. In Nebraska, where the first significant use of bales to make houses occurred, one of the oldest houses, built between 1900 and 1914, was opened up in the 1950s to allow an addition. Some of the bales were placed near a yard with horses, whereupon the horses stretched their necks over the fence and began eating the 40–50-year-old straw. In fact, the earliest bale building on record is a school built in 1886 or 87, in Scotts Bluff County, Nebraska. That school isn't around now because cattle ate it.

I had reason to think of this the other day, when Murray, the neighbour's yearling beast, clambered over my fence and came up to the house. First he chewed a few apple trees and then he wandered over to the front of the house, where it is still bare straw walls without mud. I ran out of the house flapping my arms at him. I didn't want to have to explain to the insurance agent that a steer had eaten my front wall.

When the rain set in for days, we tacked tarpaulins over the wall on the sides where the bales were closest to the weather. As the strawbale walls grew, so did the number and size of tarpaulins. Climbing up to attach the tarpaulins each night and to take them down in the morning became a major chore, one I hated because it meant heights, scaffold and ladder work again. If I could, I avoided it by being busy with another job when the time came to wrap the house up.

One afternoon Sam was finishing up the lining for the kitchen and called out to me to screw up the tarps. I took his electric drill, a handful of roof screws in my toolbelt and climbed the ladder at the front of the house to stand on the top. Even then it was a stretch for me to reach the edge of the tarp.

I was aware I was in view of the road. Here I was, a grandmother on top of a ladder with a drill I knew how to operate. Thinking how great I was, I leant out at an angle and pushed the drill hard against the beam. The sideways pressure was too much for the ladder, which shot out from underneath me. The ladder went one way and I dropped 2 metres the other way, landing on my side in the dirt. The drill went off on its own accord.

Inside, Sam was using the drop saw. It made a high-pitched whining noise, much like the one I was making down on the ground. The saw stopped and it took a moment for Sam to realise there was a strange noise still coming from outside. His footsteps thudded out of the house. He said later when he saw the ladder and me on the ground he thought the very worst.

'Jillian! Are you all right?'

I lay there groaning. Then I realised I'd landed on my butt and my iphone was in that pocket. 'Oh my God, my phone.' I scrambled up and pulled it out of my pocket. I turned it on and the screen lit up. 'That's lucky.'

'Ahh,' said Sam. 'I thought you were dying and you're just thinking about your phone.' He gave me a hug anyway. 'But what have I told you about ladder placement!'

Nothing broken, but I did get some deep bruises and a wake-up call to be more careful.

The next evening Sam called out to me again. 'Jillian, could you grab the drill and go put the tarps up?'

'I don't feel confident about doing that again,' I called back.

He came to the doorway. 'What do people say when you fall off a horse?'

A moment's silence.

'Do you want me to make allowances for you?' he asked. 'Say, don't worry, I'll do all the ladder work. You put your hand up for this, remember.'

'All right, I get it,' I said, and went and found the drill.

Before I climbed the ladder, I looked around and shifted stones and blocks of wood that I could hit my head on if I fell off again. And then I climbed up, paying attention to each step. I pressed the drill into the screw at a safe angle. I didn't like it up there, but Sam was right. It wasn't fair to load him up with jobs I was capable of doing. And it would do me no good to let fear limit my actions.

Bridget stayed on for six more days to help with the bale work. The house began to take on its shape. When we finished the wide sitting-room wall where one day the fire would go, we could see the shape of the corner window. Solidity defined space. The house smelt of macrocarpa wood and the stalky, grassy smell of straw. To walk in the house was to recall haysheds and summer grass.

The rain kept up, and the cold wind. The tarpaulins flapped and rustled over the window spaces. Rain soaked Bridget's tent and spare clothes. We wore layers of woollen clothing, hats, gloves, rain jackets, trying to keep warm on site in the windowless house. Bending and lifting the straw bales helped. When Bridget and I layered a wall up to the fifth bale again, Sam came and helped with the strops.

One afternoon Graeme came after his own day's work. 'How's it going, Team?' he called out as he came round the corner, his work gloves already on his hands. He worked with Sam setting another layer of straw into the dining-room wall. They cranked the top bales down and slid the last bale in for the night.

That week, Dennis joined us and began to lay the macrocarpa tongue-and-groove flooring above the kitchen. For the first time there was enough floor nailed down in the loft of my wall-less house to sit up there. Once we'd finished working that day, it was dark and raining. Bridget and I ran down to the pub and bought fish and chips and beer. We brought back our parcel and climbed up the ladder to Sam and Dennis. Brian had already been over and delivered every warm jacket he owned. Swathed in parkas, our fingers greasy with oil, we ate hot salty chips, while below us the house ballooned with blue tarpaulins, breathing in and out with the wind.

CHAPTER 15

The Last Photos of Our Fathers

Down the road at the old Golden Progress Mine, in a short valley that has a view to Mt St Bathans, one solitary stone cottage remains. How would the sun have got in to such a valley, and how must it have been to live winters there? I thought of that miner again with the broken arm in his freezing tent. They were cast off there from any mooring of village and home and street. They had nothing but the mountain tracks ahead of them, more wintry nights in tents, and days spent flaying the ground and the rocks for what gold they could find.

In these valleys around here the crumbling stone cottages, sometimes backed up to a hill or a rocky outcrop, leave testimony to the way people once had only their hands and the natural resources around them with which to construct shelter. For without shelter from the cold we are back in the time of Prometheus: naked, crouched people with no energy or vision to create art or music or poetry; solely concerned with how to survive.

Not quite in the primitive days of Prometheus, but Bridget and I longed for a hot shower. We asked at the pub in case they had showers to rent, but all their rooms were rented out. We knocked on Brian's door and he gave us hot cups of tea and the use of his bathroom.

Tent dwellers, vagrants; it's not long before you start to feel you live in another reality when you don't have plumbing or heating. A reality unhooked from the hyper-reality of TV, advertisements, cyber space, the news. When it all comes down to the basics of how to keep warm and how to cook food, there is a slowing down. The air and the land around you become more apparent.

When Jung built his stone house he purposely didn't allow for power or plumbing.

'I have done without electricity,' he wrote. There was no running water at his house, and he pumped the water from the well. He wrote that this simplicity in life was important, to reconnect us to our past, and to the land around us.

One night the sunset was so intense, Sam, Brian, Bridget and I took deck chairs into the damp grass by the caravan to watch it. We couldn't take our eyes off the sky. I thought of my dad, and how he would have loved to be here with us, his camera in his hand. A cloud like a dense, long-tailed dinosaur crouched over Blackstone Hill, above its back a shining egg. From the west, beyond the poplars, an array of swirling magenta clouds, and over Rough Ridge a soft haze of striated clouds. Every few minutes a change in colour, and the way the light shifted on the cloud shapes gave them a radiance. The birds sang in the darkening willows, and beneath them, the Ida Burn, full and rushy with mountain water, burbled over the stones.

In the morning, when I woke, the wild red poppies were gone. Every morning amongst the grasses they had filled their cups with sun and held their bobbing heads against the blue of Mt Ida. Wind, wind and unseasonal sleet in the night, and their petals were plastered over the grass. I thought of poet Ursula Bethell's line: 'Everything is for a very short time.'

The last time I saw my father it was early autumn. He and my stepmother Jenny had come to stay with me at my house at the beach on the Motueka Inlet. We had walked down the jiggly boards of the old boat ramp to the sand and along the tide line.

The tide was mostly in and laid a calm sheen across the sheltered bay. Along the sand bank beside us were small tufted grasses with furry heads and squashy creeping plants with bright pink centres. There was a seat a quarter of the way along the beach. Dad made it there and said he could go no further. His knee.

'You go on, I'll wait for you,' he said, but we stayed and waited with him. The water bobbled closer, making small runs in dips and hollows of the sand, and imperceptibly covering the stones and few jagged rocks in front of us. All gone, all gone, the roughness of shells, and only sea now, lively at its edge, with a ripple of foam and tiny slivers of driftwood mushing backwards and forwards near our feet.

A black-backed gull flew down from the Norfolk pine behind us. It bobbed on the water, its wings folded like a Crown Lynn swan. Sea, sky and seagull.

'Shall we have a cup of tea? I'll get the car if you need it.'

'I can walk back,' Dad said. We retraced our steps along the narrow path the tide had left us. The air smelt of salt and warm wind.

I like to think that everything I did that day was full of kindness and solicitation for my father, and that our bodies knew, or our spirits knew, even if our minds didn't, this was our last walk side by side as father and daughter.

That morning I had woken early to the sound of men's voices in the kitchen. Dave and Dad at the table, cups between them. A rare occasion. I left them to it. Later, Dave said he had asked my father for my hand, not in marriage, because he didn't believe in marriage, but in life, and my father had said, *Whatever Jillian desires*.

My father went home to his roses and his tomatoes. There was that shocking phone call; the one that shatters the illusion we are sheltered in this world or that any life is permanent.

I have a photo Jenny took that morning before we went down to the beach. 'The last photo taken of my father' I call it, and when I go to people's houses I see them there, too. My sister has one, of course, and her partner, and friends. 'This is the last photo of my father,' they tell me as they point to the frame.

That house we lived in by the beach was made from two army officers' huts from the war. They were trucked from Blenheim to the section that ran down to the sand, and put together to make one small oblong house. Someone plastered them over, cementing the idea of a home. Not an ugly home, but a plain, squat house with low-pitched roof; a house that shrugged off any attempt at betterment.

The architect Min Hall came round for an hour's consultation on what could be done on our small budget to improve the house. She walked all through it and told us only to shift the fireplace to an interior wall and put in doors to the garden.

'The house is unpretentious,' she said. 'A house of six rooms. It's so exactly what it is, just leave it like that.' So we did.

Even the roofer who came to give a quote wouldn't replace the roof.

'Just paint it,' he said. 'That tough old iron has years left in it.'

I sanded and painted the roof, up there looking over the doings of the sea and the birds. On the beach is the seat Dad rested on, and the sea still forever bringing its daily gifts of driftwood and shell to the sand. The gulls strut up and down on the shore, which is home to them, and food basket, this shore much more theirs than ours.

In spring, though I am here in the deepest south, with the Merinos fresh and white from the shearing shed, the bar-tailed godwits will return to that shore as they do every spring, wheeling and banking and turning in the sky over the Kumaras estuary like an airborne school of fish. They'll come to rest in the reeds, the patterns of migration, their seaward homes, imprinted under their wings. They know where they must go and where they must return to, their sense of home unerring across continents, across oceans.

CHAPTER 16

An End to Straw

Bridget had gone back to Nelson. I stood in the house with its empty walls and the stacks of straw in the sitting room, bedroom and bathroom. I looked around at all that had to be done. The house looked more like a shed than a home. Outside in the paddock the yarrow had gone brown and to seed. The early mist on the Home Hills, in front of the Hawkduns, had burnt off. Another hot day ahead, and the long grass and the yarrow bending in the wind.

On bale-raising day, the energy of everyone around and the sense of things being achieved made the project fun, as if it was the best thing to do in the world. Now Sam had left me alone with bales to sew to the window frames, while he chiselled out the beams for the loft. Once more I doubted my abilities.

When we were building the timber structure, I felt secure knowing Sam had everything under control and knew what needed to be done. All I had to do was follow his direction. Now we both had to figure out how to get the bales in and finish the house.

I picked up the raspy, textured baling needle, threaded it, and put my shoulder into pushing the needle through the bale.

What had I done? How was this shed going to be a house?

And more frightening, the funds from the mortgage I had arranged were going out faster than I had anticipated. Would the house even get finished to live in? Perhaps it would stay like this, a shed of straw, for years. And then what?

There were 30 straw bales stacked beside me in what was supposed to be a bathroom. My one night's sleep in here had felt part of a marvellous adventure. Now even the music was morose. I pulled the needle back through the bale and tied the baling twine tight around the window frame.

'Sam, I'm changing the music,' I called out. We normally took turns having our choice of music on. I ducked under the 4×2 bracing the doorway. In the sitting room I flicked the iPod onto The Animals. The seven-high stack of bales loomed over me. Nick was gone, too.

Sam looked up from the long macrocarpa beam he was working on. It spanned two sawhorses and was a third of the width of the house. Around him, the sweet-smelling sawdust of macrocarpa.

'Good choice of music,' he said. 'How's the sewing?'

'It's all right,' I said. 'What about you?'

'I'm loving it. Just getting amongst it here with Big French.'

'With what?'

He held his chisel out, and I took the weight of the wooden handle.

'My friend brought it back from France for me. I asked him to buy the biggest chisel he could find. He gave it to me engraved and named.'

I passed Big French back to him. I liked the idea of a tool with its own name.

'It's just so good to be working with hand tools, doing something that takes skill and craft for a change instead of firing a nail gun. You know this type of joint, a mortise and tenon joint, has a history of over a thousand years. But now we've got nails and fixings, people don't pay you to do this sort of work anymore.'

I looked at him.

'You'll appreciate it, looking up at the ceiling and only seeing beams,' he said.

'I'm happy for you, Sam. How many more notches do you have to chisel?'

'Six each side, 12 on each beam, that's 20 to go now.'

I nodded. Back to my sewing. I threaded up my bale needle, leant my shoulder to the straw.

I know when writing a novel, it's not the beginning that's difficult. This is the stage when you are full of desire to write, when the story seems vibrant, the characters arise and you hear their voices for the first time.

It's not the end that's difficult either, because by then you are in a headlong rush. Everything has come together; you know how it's going to turn out. You love your novel all over again, and even if you are on bloodied knees, with a knife between your teeth as you crawl up that last path to the finish, there is depth behind you. All those lives, all those stories, all those nights and cold mornings of writing about to be over.

It's in the middle where all seems lost. The story loses momentum, the characters stare blankly at the wall, the whole thing appears boring and you realise you have given up a career, sleep, social outings with friends, laziness, reading great books by other writers, all to write this stuff on your pages, which will probably never sell and be yet another dream that didn't come to fruition. The middle – that's the part we want to avoid.

I pulled the needle through the bale and tied the baling twine tight. This twine embedded in the straw bale and looped around the window frame would help hold the wall in place until the mud, and then the lime plaster, encased everything in a hardened shell. Two strings on the post done. Three more to do for that height of window. Five more to do the other side of the window. Eight windows to go. Nineteen more posts. On the edge of my vision a mouse ran deliriously towards the bale stack.

Peter Jackson said once in an interview he reached that tortuous 'middle' stage during filming of *The Lord of the Rings*. He doubted his vision. He had a cast and workers by the hundreds working on a film he himself had lost hope in. And then he kept going. He pushed through to make his film. When I read that, I thought, even Peter Jackson feels like that? And if he could make a trilogy, then I could at least finish whatever story I was working on. Or house.

I knew this about middles, and I knew Sam and I would keep on working as long as we could. I didn't say anything to Sam, but a few months later in May, when Sven came to show us how to put mud on, he expressed how I'd been feeling by saying, 'You love seeing the straw when it first goes in the walls, and you love seeing it get covered up.'

Yes, I wanted an end to straw, to the 'shedness' of the house, and to the mice who thought this was a new kind of heaven on earth for them, planted down in winter.

The morning it was so cold the bananas froze in the caravan, Sam came up to me where I was cutting wood on the drop saw. We both had gloves and hats on. The wind came straight off Blackstone Hill, chilled with snow.

'I'm just about over all this,' Sam said.

Of course it was harder for him. He missed Hana and the children.

I stood looking across the paddock, desperately wondering what to say to him. The tussock, the broom and the rye grass were stilled by the white. Mt Ida, a stark shoulder, and behind it the sky lemon, blue and lightening. In the bale garden beside me, the kale and silverbeet were topped with frost crystals. How could we keep camping in this climate? I looked over my frozen vegetable garden at the house next door. Oh, but the tenants had moved out the week before!

'Sam, I'll rent a house,' I said. I pulled out my phone and rang the young guy who owned it, Shane Clarke. Though he hadn't met me before, he told me where the key was.

'Can we move in right now?' I asked.

'Sure. There's firewood in the shed.'

Fire. Hot bath. Flushing toilet. An oven to cook in. Even a washing machine. Work waited while Sam and I rushed from room to room exclaiming at the sheer space of a house after the caravan. Plumbing! Electricity! Sam lit the fire.

That house would keep us going for the next six weeks as winter set in. And now, with a warm place to stay, Hana and the children could come over to be with Sam sometimes.

I'd bought an old weedeater for trimming the straw walls. They needed a straw haircut so they would have regular sides to take the mud plaster. Though I spent $200 on the weedeater, it wasn't up to the job. Dennis lent us his grunty one, and he arrived on the Tuesday to help Sam trim the walls. The men took turns to move the weedeater in large arcs over the face of the straw bales, shaving them straight. I raked up the wispy trimmings of straw and stored them in large sacks to use later for making mud mix for the walls.

In the middle of the straw-trimming task, on a fine, cold afternoon, a covered truck pulled up on site, bringing the wooden joinery. Declan had arrived to help, and he and Brian and Dennis helped Sam and I lift the heavy timber windows off the truck and carry them into the house.

I don't know how we started talking about love with the truck driver who delivered the windows. Perhaps Declan asked him if he was married. The driver was tall, gap-toothed and craggy-faced.

'Not married, but I've been with my beautiful partner for four years now,' he said.

'How did you meet her?' I asked.

'I was shifting furniture for a friend of hers and she was helping. She got my phone number off the side of the truck. Next thing I get a text: *You look a kind man. Come for dinner 7 tonight at my place.*

I thought she sounded brave, and resourceful.

'I texted back: *Shall I bring my toothbrush or a bottle of wine.*'

We all laughed.

'Then what?' I asked. 'Then what did she say?'

'Aw, I wouldn't really turn up on my first date with a toothbrush,' he said. 'I didn't mean that. But we've been together ever since.'

The house filled with straw, windows in, the lower level trimmed ready for mud.

We stood and waved when he drove the lumbering truck out of the section. I thought of how the woman in his story made the first move, copying down his phone number and ringing him. And he had to be brave, too, to say yes.

Declan came back for the third time to work on the straw walls. Nick came again in his holidays and helped with getting the bales in the difficult apex of the house. Rory, my eldest son, came to help with the upstairs flooring and to build the curved window heads.

While the walls could be stacked with straw bales in a brick pattern, one on top of the other, above the window there was no frame to support a straw bale. Instead, Rory and I mimicked the depth of a bale by creating a stuffed straw fixture. We used rubber-backed underlay, tacking it onto the beam that supported the roof truss and again just above the window. Rory and I stuffed in straw and thumped it and compressed it with the handle of the hammer. We held the underlay tight and tacked some more up, then pushed in and compressed more straw, repeating this over and over to make a tightly packed, curved structure above the window. Once the underlay was plastered, it would look the same as the walls made of bales.

Out of chaos, and what had looked like a barn, bales became walls. There was an end to the empty spaces where wind blew. There were four walls and windows of glass so now we could see the mountains instead of tarpaulins.

Once again everything seemed possible. There would be mud.

PART THREE

EARTH

Bringing nothing more than my hands to the task, I slowly rubbed and pressed the wood as if it were muscled flesh, over and over again in a widening spiral of attention. And after a few hours it did begin to feel like some weird interspecies form of massage.

– MICHAEL POLLAN, *A PLACE OF MY OWN: THE EDUCATION OF AN AMATEUR BUILDER,* 1997

CHAPTER 17

Mud Daze

L et's talk about mice.

My main reservation about building with straw wasn't to do with moisture, councils or the unknowingness of the building process, it was the mice. Or worse, rats. No book I read really addressed this subject, except one which said you must immediately seal the bales with plaster to stop rodents getting in. That was always my plan, but of course that didn't happen when all the bales didn't go in on the first day and mud plaster did not immediately follow that night.

For the 180-square-metre house we helped on at Geraldine, the plasterer said it would take him five months to finish plastering the house inside and out. Five months? I thought mine would be completed in a day. I actually believed that, and when it came time to make up the mud plaster, I calculated how much I would need for the inside and outside of the house, *six cubic metres*, and made the whole lot at once. The mud had to ferment for three to five days before mud-plastering day, so I wanted to make sure I had enough ready for the whole house.

When Sven turned up to run a workshop for Sam, Declan and me, he'd looked at the gigantic pit of mud I'd made.

'I've never seen so much earth plaster made up before,' he said.

Really? So this wasn't normal? It was hard to work out what was normal when none of us had worked with straw before.

Well, the straw bales didn't all go in in one day, and the mud didn't go on in one day either. In fact, I ended up living in the house all winter with the front wall and the two gable sections of the walls unplastered, and the rest of the house needing one more coat of mud plaster. Immediate application of mud was never going to happen for this project. Which left me with the mice.

As soon as the bales were stored inside the house for that first night of rain, there were mice. I set traps, which they just ran past on their way to the treasure trove of barley seeds that filtered out of the straw.

I've never coped well with mice. When Evie had two pet mice at the age of four, she used to keep them in her dress pockets. The whole time she owned mice I didn't touch them once, though she would hold them up to me. They do have bright eyes and an inquisitive face. Saying this doesn't help when I go to set more traps. Perhaps it is a phobia.

Then everything I dreaded about rodents in a strawbale house looked like it was going to come true. Mice ran up the walls. They came through them. One day the electrician, working halfway up the wall to get a cable in, heard a squeaking. Right by his face, a mouse flew out the wall.

What would happen when the mud plaster went on? Would mice be trapped in the walls, roaming around, breeding, so that the walls became infested, seething mouse gangs within the house. Would the mice survive?

'I've seen a mouse eat its way out of an earthen-plastered wall,' Sven said when I asked him. 'But I've never heard of a mouse eating its way back in.'

That was some consolation.

I went down to the shop to talk to Rhonda. 'The mice take no notice of my traps,' I said.

'You have to keep putting poison out,' she said. 'Sprinkle it in the corners. Everyone does that round here, especially the houses that are locked up for winter.'

Not only did mice scuttle into the house, but birds flew directly into my walls and disappeared. That winter Declan found a hole in the front wall where we still hadn't sealed it with mud, and inside were twenty sparrows bundled up against the snowy air.

After a while I became almost used to the mice as we worked. The only real fright I got was when I crouched down to put mud on a gap between the wall and the floor, and a mouse ran straight out at my eyes. I yelled out.

'They won't hurt you,' Sam called back. I filled the hole with mud, and everywhere else mice found entranceways, I plugged with mud.

Sam was working next to a wall covered in plaster when a mouse ran at the wall and attempted to run up it, as the mice used to do when the wall was straw. The mouse fell down onto the ground, ran up and fell, ran up and fell, and then sat there at Sam's feet, looking at the wall, probably thinking, 'What the *#**?'

A report now from living in the house with the exterior walls mostly sealed: the only mice I see is about one every two weeks in the trap in winter. And that is very fine with me.

When it came to making plaster, this time I had a mentor drop in to see me beforehand and give me a run through. Greg Tump used to be a builder and now specialises in earthen plastering. I'd hoped to pay him to come for a week to prepare the clay needed for the mud mix and to teach us how to plaster. He couldn't. He was working on a big project, he said, and couldn't spare even a Saturday. But he called in to give me some advice on his way back from Dunback, a place about an hour past me over the Pigroot and the only place in the South Island to sell burnt lime for the finish coat of lime plastering.

First Greg walked around looking at our strawbale walls, now and then thumping them. He was pleased with the strength and firmness of their compression. I showed him the steel plates we had designed for compressing the walls. He showed me his arbour tech grinder he preferred to use to cut the bales instead of chainsawing the straw.

For an hour he ran me through what I needed to do on site before plastering and how to make the mud plaster. I wrote notes on an offcut of wood.

I was to plug holes in the straw walls by twisting lengths of straw, stuffing them in the gaps between bales, then pounding them in with a blunt stick, or as I came to use, the handle of my hammer. I was to cover all the posts, beams and bracing straps with a watered-down tile adhesive for the mud to stick to. (Later we abandoned this procedure as Sven said it would work without it, and it did.) Stucco netting had to be nailed for 200 mm down from each top beam into the straw to mesh the beams and straw together. A slip coat had to be sprayed on the straw first. This was a mixture of really fine sifted clay and water we made up in a drum. We mixed the clay and water with an electric drill and paddle, and blasted the slip on with a compressor.

'You'll need about six cubic metres of clay, get a truckload,' Greg said. 'Same of gravel dust. Then you'll need fine straw; you can mow it with a lawnmower.' (I had the clipped straw from Sam weedeating the walls.) 'And non-toxic sawdust. Get a big drum for water to speed up the mixing. Construct a pit to put the mud plaster in for fermenting, get a concrete mixer, and get everything piled in the same area. Here will work,' and he walked around a flat area behind the house, pointing out to me, 'Here,' for the pile of clay, 'and here,' for the gravel dust.

'How will I sift the clay?' I asked him. I'd been relying on the fact he would come and do the job for me and bring his own heavy equipment. The clay needed to be sifted to make sure the particles in it were less than 4 mm so they would mix easily.

'You could borrow one of those large mulchers,' he said. 'The ones you tow behind your car.'

The clay arrives on site.

And this was the recipe for each concrete-mixer load: 20 kilos of sifted clay (not any clay, it had to be sticky clay; there was a quarry near Clyde somewhere), 20 kilos of gravel dust, the same amount of straw (half of it long straw, half of it chopped-up straw, all packed tightly in a bucket), water about the same, enough to mix, and 10 kilos of sawdust. If no sawdust, shredded paper that had been soaked overnight.

It was an approximate recipe of 1:1:1:5. How much water depended on all sorts of things and was something I would have to figure out. I'd never seen plastering mud being made before. I had no idea what it was supposed to look like or feel like.

At night I lay in bed thinking, what if I get the mixture completely wrong? What if it doesn't work on the straw? The safety of my whole house depended on me making an earthen plaster, and what if it didn't work? My house would rot. I had spent all this money, all this time, and then I'd be in a pit up to my knees in mud I didn't know how to make.

Sam had to be home for the weekend. Their house was for sale and he had things to finish. He gave me the task of getting the clay sifted in the weekend. I looked at the huge pile in the backyard. Eight cubic metres, a truck had delivered. Somehow that would be sifted by Monday morning, ready to start making plaster.

To hire a mulcher meant a two-hour return journey and $150. I backed the mulcher onto the site near the clay. Soon I had it set up, with tarpaulins spread out ready to catch the finely sifted material. Petrol in it. Push the button to start. A heartening roar. I scooped in the first few shovelfuls of clay. They didn't subtract so much as a pinprick of clay from the pile in front of me. Never mind. 'Continuous effort – not strength or intelligence – is the key ...' as Winston Churchill said.

The mulcher spat the fine clay out two metres into the air. I didn't appreciate till later there was a pipe I could adjust to direct the mulched clay onto the ground. About the tenth shovelful, the mulcher stopped working. I turned it off and peered in. The whole top of the hopper was filled with clay and the blades weren't working. I tried poking things in to move the clay about. I tried scooping it out with my hands. I turned the mulcher on again and it still didn't work. A fine Saturday morning, a massive pile of clay to sift, no mulcher, and at the worst, I might have wrecked it.

I rang Sam.

'I can't do anything to help from here,' he said. 'Give Graeme Male a ring, he might know.'

I rang Graeme. He didn't know about mulchers.

'Give Brian a ring,' he said. I rang Brian, and even though he was at his desk working, he came down with some tools, and we both peered in the hopper.

The first hour we tried cleaning it with the machine intact. After that Brian took it to pieces. We brushed out every bit of clay. Put the machine back together again. I put some pine branches through the mulcher to clean any trace of gritty clay out and to check it was working. The mulcher spat the chopped-up pine branches with force straight at the outside toilet wall. It worked fine. Probably the lightest work the machine had had in a weekend for years. The next day I drove the two-hour return journey to take the mulcher back.

On Monday morning Sam turned up back at work and looked at the pile of unsifted clay.

'Now what?' he said.

'Well, the truck driver told me he ran the digger back and forth over the clay to break it up before he loaded it. I think it might be ok as it is.' We both took handfuls and let it fall through our fingers.

A new friend I'd made in Queenstown drove over to help me start on my first ever batch of mud. Antonia Cooney is an interior designer. She's in her forties, with long blonde hair. She turned up in her black VW Golf with a vegetable quiche and a bottle of champagne. She had lipstick on, and when it came time to start making mud plaster, pulled on a pair of designer floral gumboots she'd bought in Melbourne. Making mud with style.

Having her there, another woman beside me, gave me the confidence to start on the recipe.

We made the first concrete-mixer load. The 20-litre buckets of clay and gravel were too heavy for either of us to lift on our own so we lifted the buckets together. We peered into the mixer as it galumphed around, checking the mud mix like anxious cooks.

I took a handful of mud and smeared it through my palms. Though the pile of clay looked like it was fine enough, once shovelfuls went into the mixer, bigger lumps became apparent. They hadn't mixed in with the straw and sawdust, but resolutely stayed clay.

'I'm going to have to sift the clay somehow,' I said. 'With something.'

I ran down to the caravan and shed, to the pile of odd things Sam had brought across when he was emptying out his garage at home.

When he began as an adult apprentice builder, his boss, with a new house to start, would first load up the truck with a pile of 'rubbish' and take it to the new site. Sam didn't understand why the boss would take old crap to a new house. And then he learnt it was in the crap that you found the bits and pieces you needed.

'No point going down to PlaceMakers to buy a piece of timber so you can use some of it and make the rest rubbish,' said Sam, passing on the wisdom. So he'd brought rubbish over to my place. I hunted through piles of old timber, lengths of steel and gardening pots, and picked up a white plastic supermarket tray that must have been used for bananas. It still had the Dole label on the front. It had rigid sides and a mesh bottom that looked the right size for sifting clay.

I came back with it to Antonia. We placed it over a bucket, I shovelled some clay into it, picked it up and shook it, and voilà! Fine clay in the bucket, perfect for the mixer. We worked for four hours and at the end had a small pile of mud in one corner of the wooden pit. Declan had made the pit out of old pallets and lined it with tarpaulin. A pit big enough to fit 6 cubic metres of mud. Obviously this mud-making was going to take a whole lot longer than I had anticipated.

Sam came out to have a look how we were doing.

'Is this mix all right?' I asked him.

'I don't know. It looks all right to me,' he said.

Antonia left at sunset. The sky began to light up with fiery shades of scarlet and gold over the black outline of Blackstone Hill. The concrete mixer rumbled and thrummed. The mud in the twilight smelling of the puggy edge of a pond. I grappled another bucket of sand to tip into the mixer. The sun flung a last outrageous red onto the underbellies of clouds, and changed through magenta to purple and the deepening sky of night.

Sam came out with a builder's lamp and set it on a box for me. He went back to work into the night on the loft and I carried on in the cold, heaving the buckets up in stages to tip into the mixer. I could see the clay and sand and sawdust and straw but not into the pit to check the texture of my mix.

At 9 p.m. I stopped for the night. The pile of mud in the pit didn't look much higher than it had at 4 p.m. I wrapped my cold arms around my chest. All that effort for such a small heap. It was like that moment when you hike to what you think is the top of a mountain range, only to see a vista of higher peaks stretching away from you.

Some relief came in the form of unemployment. Rory's job as financial analyst in Wellington ended when Telecom stripped 1500 workers of their jobs. He flew down south to help me, and there we were for a week, a mother and son playing with mud as if it were playgroup again.

After a week of making mud, and putting in windows with Rory, Brian, Declan and Dennis to help, Sam and I began on the inside walls. He cut and fitted gib sheets to the interior framing. Later he would staple old carpet, with the hessian (coarse) side out onto the gib, and I would plaster it with the mud mix. Eventually all the interior walls would match the exterior mud walls in texture, the earth plaster adding temperature and sound insulation.

'Don't gib that wall next to the toilet yet,' I told Sam. 'I want to soundproof it.'

'We haven't any insulation batts on site,' he said. 'You don't need it in there.'

'It's the wall between the toilet and the sitting room,' I said. 'Of course I want insulation. It's all right, I'll make it myself.'

'Just don't take too long. I need your help with the gib.'

'I won't. Twenty minutes I'll be there.'

I went out to the concrete mixer and studied my piles of ingredients. Perhaps if I made a really thick, strawy batch of mud, I could plaster that inside the framing of the wall. I started alternating a bucket of clay with a bucket of straw, then

With son Rory and six cubic metres of mud.

another bucket of straw. The mix flumped around in the mixer and didn't bind. I tipped it out into a 20-litre bucket and mixed it by hand.

It didn't stick in the wall frames the way I imagined. The mud was so heavy it peeled off the wall.

'Are you finished yet?' Sam called.

'No. I need more time.'

I looked around the hallway at the boxes of building things. There were a few empty beer bottles. I'd seen bottles put in a house in *Grand Designs* on TV. I jammed bottles into the mix and pinned the mud back into the frame. Then I found old strips of carpet, old rubber gloves, some of the insulation tubes that had covered the pipes. I crammed them into the wall and held them in with mud from the bucket beside me.

'Ok,' called Sam, 'I need to gib that wall.' He came into the bathroom. He stared at my artistic creation of insulation.

'What do you think?' I asked him.

He walked out of the room. In a few minutes he was back with a box of assorted holey gloves, a wrecked shoe, more bottles and carpet.

'Move over,' he said. 'It's my turn to get amongst it.'

We plastered his collection into the frames as well, checking out each other's style. Insulation completed.

Sam glued and screwed the aqualine gib sheet onto the framing, hiding perhaps forever our sculptural creation.

'Let's try it out,' I said. 'You first.' I went through into the sitting room while Sam stayed in the toilet making loud noises.

'I can't hear you! Oh, ok, I can. But not much.'

Then we went back to gibbing.

After work, Sam rode his bike up onto Rough Ridge. He was in training for the Motatapu mountain bike race. I pulled on a jersey and sat on a straw bale on the verandah. Even the grass had gone to seed, the tall spears of timothy and cocksfoot swayed with grain. In the willows by the pond the sparrows chirped. To the right, the rocky tors along the skyline of Rough Ridge mellowed with golden light.

A flock of sparrows lifted from the long grass and hurled themselves about in a joyousness of flight. The birds looked like thick-bodied butterflies, or long-winged bees. I felt a calmness, a quietness inside, sitting there and watching them. There was no other place I wanted to be than right there, on a warm verandah, birds and grasses and mountains in the cool, clear air. And I knew that was because, with help, I was rebuilding myself here, with each nail that was hammered home, with each bale that raised the walls. Over Blackstone Hill the sunset blazed.

CHAPTER 18

An Interweaving Story

The clay/sand/sawdust/straw mix works best when it is left for three to five days, plasterer Greg had told me. It gives the straw a chance to start fermenting. A chemical change takes place in the straw and it becomes, instead of a stalky substance, a pliable one that acts like a glue holding the mud-mix together. Some batches I made, even some areas of the mud pit, were better than others, and gave me a silky, gluey mixture to work with. When I finally got to the task of smearing the mud on the straw, it was nothing short of a sensuous, tactile experience, and one where hours went by without stopping for food or drink and I hardly noticed. Lost in the bliss, the mindfulness of mud.

I set the mud-plastering day for 20 April, 2013. Like the strawbale-raising day, this day would be an occasion for people to come together and help on the project. The Bridgets couldn't come this time. Julie would be there, though, taking charge of grandchildren and the food. Nick and Bex were coming from Auckland. Graeme Male would be there, and this time Grahame Sydney would come as well. Dennis couldn't be there for mud day.

Dennis came during the week instead to help again with the flooring. He and Rory crouched together up in the loft as Dennis showed Rory how to work the drop saw, how to fit the macrocarpa tongue-and-groove lengths together, how to clamp them, how to rule straight lines for nail holes and nail them in neatly. Plank by plank the floor above the kitchen and dining room evolved.

Seeing Dennis teach Rory to build was one of the highlights of the house project for me. It showed me that building a house can be a way for families to come back and connect. It's a chance for wiser, more skilled people to pass on their knowledge, and not just about building. All sorts of things were discussed and worked out amidst the hammering.

And it occurred to me that many of the people who came to work on the house were at some transitional phase in their lives. Maybe coming together to build was not only helping me get a footing, but a way for others to rebuild their lives.

Pat Shuker came twice more to work on the house. She said after the first time, even though she had worked hard for two days, she drove away feeling 20 years younger. When she told a friend she was coming back to help with the mud, her friend asked her, 'Why are you going all that way to help someone you don't really know?'

'I said to her,' Pat told me, 'I can't have my own dream of a strawbale house yet, so I want to help someone else get theirs. That's what you do, my generation anyway. If someone needs a hand, you get in and help them.'

And Pat took her work seriously, too. Usually on Sundays at home, Sam would get up early to make Hana and the children a big cooked breakfast. He decided to do this on a Sunday morning at the rented house when Pat was staying to help.

'Stay in bed, Pat,' he called, 'and I'll bring you breakfast in bed.'

'That's not going to happen,' said Pat, emerging from her room at 7 a.m., fully dressed for work. She walked out the front door and straight over to the site.

When I went looking for her, she was up a ladder with a bucket of mud plaster and straw, dealing with the hole in the wall she'd been working on yesterday. In some places, especially around window frames, we hadn't chainsawed the straw bales snugly enough. There were deep crevices in the straw wall that needed filling with copious amounts of mud and straw. If we didn't do that, the top coat of mud plaster fell out because the base behind it wasn't firm enough.

'I was lying in bed last night thinking how I could fix this gap,' said Pat, 'and I think I've got it sorted.'

I scooped myself a bucket of mud and went to work beside her. She watched me folding pieces of straw over to jam into holes.

'Here, I'll show you something I learnt in Africa.' She'd lived there for years and volunteered for a doctor from Médecins Sans Frontières. She helped out in the villages, not just with health but with housing. 'Put two handfuls of straw together,' she showed me. 'This is what the women in the village taught me. Now tease the straw out, like teasing wool to spin. This way you've got a longer, thinner hunk of straw. Bend it over, twist it, bend it over, twist it. That's right. Now push it in the wall.'

Rory, who has strengths in project management, had taken one look at my slow progress making mud when he first arrived, looked at the sifter on top of the bucket and said, 'I can't stand this.' He walked around the site with the intense gaze of a searchlight. Within a few minutes he had assembled a bench made out of two stacks of straw bales, two-high, with the sifter in the middle and a tarp underneath. Now faster work could take place. Much easier to shovel clay into the sifter and keep sifting into the space below than to position the sifter over a bucket.

Sifting became a two-person speedy job. Rory took to it with the ferocious energy he puts into any work he does. Six cubic metres of mud mix? Coming right up.

Rory and I worked on into the night again. When Brian came over and helped for a while, the mixer loads pumped out. I shovelled the clay into the sifter, Brian sifted, Rory threw the 20-litre bucketfuls of ingredients into the mixer. I ran round and loaded straw into the buckets or refilled the drum with water when needed.

When the concrete mixer had turned the ingredients from a wet/stalky/sloppy mess into a malleable creamy-textured mud, Rory heaved the mixer over and tipped it out into the pit. Sometimes I had to clamber into the pit with a grubber to push the mud out of the way and to make way for the next loads.

'Do you think the mud looks all right?' I asked Sam again as he walked past.

'I don't know what it should look like,' he said. 'It looks good to me.'

In two days' time Rory and I had the pit full of mud. Six cubic metres of it. We crossed tarpaulins over the mud, tucked it up against rain and ice and let it do its fermenting thing. In the night I stressed about the wetness of it. Water had pooled across the top of the mud. Was it too wet? Would it fall off the walls? Would it ever set?

I rang Sven. Sven had said he'd be able to come and spend a day with us plastering. He couldn't make it on the Saturday, but could come the day before. He would teach us and Declan could film him, and we would teach anyone who came.

'I'm scared the mix is too wet,' I told him on the phone.

'Whatever it looks like, we'll fix it on the day,' he said.

And at that, my worries ceased. So mud plaster was fixable? And someone who knew what they were doing would supervise the mix and show us how to put it on.

I was right about the pools of water on top of the mud. The mix was far too wet.

'Goodness,' Sven said, looking at the several inches of water sitting on top of the mud. 'Let some water drain out, and we'll put loads back through the mixer before we use it.'

He leant over and scooped ten, fifteen shovelfuls of mud into the mixer. We watched it tumble until Sven was pleased with the consistency. He took a handful and turned his hand upside down. The mud stayed stuck to his palm.

'That's what we're after,' he said. 'This is a beautiful sticky mix.'

He took a wheelbarrow load over to the house, and in a flick of an eye, he was covering up the straw. A whole new phase in the house had begun. He worked swiftly, talking to us all the while.

'Slap it on with force,' he said, 'and keep your hand on it, don't lift your hand up, that will suck the mud back off again. Rub it in to the straw. Now another handful. That's right, slap it on. It can go quite fast from here.'

Sam and I had prepared the walls by spraying on the slip mixture, the clay and water mix. It had dried on the straw and left a rough surface for the mud to bond to.

Finally it was my turn to apply mud. I scooped a handful of the goopy mixture and slapped it against the straw. I kept my hand pressed against the wall and moved it in circles, the silky mud like wet bread dough against my palm, between my fingers. I took more handfuls, the mud warm from the sun, and fleshed out my first section of wall.

To begin with the mud plaster was uneven, yet as I passed my hand over and over it, as if the wall was an animal I caressed, the mud became sleek, the joins between handfuls seamless. My house began to transform under my fingers; not shed, but home. I plastered with the sun on my back, pressing and squidging the mud into the straw. All the work up till now – the digging, the timber work, the long, long days of fitting bales in walls – seemed just the prelude and now the house began. Smooth sides, malleable contours, the shapes and shades of straw now one colour, one texture. The mud had a power I hadn't imagined. Such a lovely mix of broken down straw, wet dirt, pulpy sawdust and sand. Plastering became an act of alchemy.

The next morning, friends and family gathered for Mud Day. Up and down the scaffolds and around the house, with trowels or bare hands, with buckets and wheelbarrows, we continued the process of transformation. Only Phoenix, aged two, declared he didn't like mud, and unlike the rest of us, stayed clean.

'The more of the building we do ourselves,' wrote Charles Goodrich in his book *The Practice of Home*, 'the more we interpenetrate with tools and ideas, with neighbours and values, merchants and ethics, birds and ambitions, governments and poetry, lumber, weather, curiosity and bugs.'

A family affair in the mud factory.

It reminded me of how the birds and mice penetrated my house when it was just timber and straw. The birds flew straight into the straw wall; one minute they were flying, the next they'd disappeared. And several times a mouse suddenly leapt out of the wall from halfway up, like Super Mouse, and landed on the floor and ran away. The weather penetrated us. The sun swatted at us.

'What do you think? 40 degrees today?' I'd ask Sam. We knew the weather intimately, on the backs of thighs, our forearms and necks. Later we knew the mud intimately as well. I knew it with my feet and ankles (scratched to bleeding by the gravel component as I trampled), with my knees, when I was knee-deep in mud. And all of us knew mud on our hands and arms and faces, in our eyes and in our mouths.

'Taste it,' a man from up north said, visiting the site from the cafe. 'That's how you'll tell if it's the right silkiness for plastering.'

I felt the mud on my lips and tongue, the smoothness of it. And we all felt the

And on it goes.

rough of the straw as we rubbed mud into it, the mud interpenetrating the straw, and our hands, too – arms sometimes deep in crevices that needed stuffing – so that the whole process of building was this interweaving: macrocarpa dust in our eyes and mouths, and our blood on the hammer and on our shins onto timber, and ladders up through beams in the airy loft, or climbing up the framing, so that we were in and through and between and on top of the structure that would eventually become my home.

One night in early May, plastering inside with Sam, it became apparent we would run out of mud mixture in a few days. I went outside and stood by the mud pit. Above me, a cloudless, darkening sky. Though I had a woollen hat and jersey on and a rain jacket and gloves, I couldn't keep the cold wind from chilling me. The thought of heaving 10-litre buckets full of gravel and clay in the dark by myself for a few hours seemed daunting. I looked up the driveway, as if by wanting and wishing, someone would arrive to help me.

Once before, help had come. I'd looked up the drive one afternoon, wishing for someone, and a big ute drove in at that exact moment. Angela Wilson, a rural woman from up the valley, had called in to have another go at putting on mud.

'I have to *make* mud today. Do you feel like doing that instead?'

'Sure,' she'd said. 'Whatever helps most.' And so her strong arms helped lift the buckets and we both peered into the concrete mixer, like the experienced country cooks that we were, to watch our mixture tumble.

But no help this time.

I began to shovel clay. Tipped it through the sifter. Lifted it back up into the concrete mixer. Handfuls of straw into the bucket. Scraped around for the last of the sawdust. Lugged the gravel buckets over and steeled myself to lift them up to the mixer's drum.

I watched the grey shape of the mixer tumbling. And there, standing in the dark on the frosty ground, I remembered it was the tenth of May, the day my father had died, 11 years earlier. My father had been a plasterer all his life. And now I was. I looked up at the cold and starry sky.

Here I am, Dad. I'm making mud.

I wheeled the first load towards the house.

CHAPTER 19

A Way Home

A car and trailer pulled up by my fence line. I ran across the paddock through the knee-deep brown yarrow to open the gate for Brian. He was on a firewood mission. There was snow on Mt Ida, and a light covering on Blackstone Hill and Rough Ridge, but nothing really serious yet. Hold off, please, the worst of winter. Brian began to chainsaw a fallen willow branch by the pond. I carried armloads of pale lemon logs up to the trailer and then headed back to the house and my job, mudding round the kitchen window.

Over Mt Ida, the clouds were thick and yellow. The tussock waved in the wind, but not like yesterday. The wind had thumped us yesterday. The big tarpaulin over the precious clay had bucked and flapped and Sam and I had gone round putting extra lumps of wood on it to hold it down.

With the short time left for Sam and I to work together, less than two weeks, we'd made decisions on what was vital to be done. The front wall of the house was bare straw, yet safely covered by the deep verandah. We left plastering that wall for the coming summer. Mud had to be completed on the inside walls so I could move in, at least one coat everywhere, and two for the kitchen area for a start. The unplumbed ensuite was more of an indoor shed for tools. We left those walls bare straw till summer as well.

Sometimes people came and helped with the laborious first coats in the bedrooms and sitting room. The first coat is where all the dips and valleys in the bale walls become apparent. It takes handfuls and handfuls of mud to straighten out each small area.

Declan brought his teenage girls to help plaster one bedroom wall. I liked knowing young people were able to experience the hands-on job of making a house. The mud was icy cold, however, from out in its pit in the chilly air, and our hands soon became numb. We were far too close to winter to be doing inside mud. The rooms now had a wet, cave-like appearance. No more golden straw;

instead, dark grey walls and a damp earth smell. I'm not sure that was the best inspiration for teenage girls.

Sam and I began work in the afternoon putting wool batts in the ceiling. I'd thought about buying the cheaper pink batts, but Sam said, 'It's a natural house, put natural batts into it.' And also, he pointed out, as I wouldn't have money for ceilings, I could live for a year or so with exposed wool batts above my head but not fibreglass batts shedding microscopic glass.

As it turned out, I didn't have money for any kind of batts.

'I can live without insulation for a while,' I'd told Sam.

'Not in this climate,' he said. 'Not in an unfinished house in minus 15–20 degrees.' Instead, he and Hana bought the woollen batts, $3000 worth. In return I could work it off, two days a week, on the next houses Sam built. I would be his builder's mate again.

The week before, I'd had to ring the plumber, Quentin, who lives in Queenstown, and tell him I couldn't employ him anymore (or any other tradesmen). The outgoings on the house had escalated, the money coming in had stopped when my job ended, and one night, in the clear light of facts, I'd faced there wasn't enough money to finish the house. Not even to get running water inside.

'I'm so grateful for my fire and wetback,' I said to Quentin. 'And there's the outside tap. I'll be all right for quite a while. I'm just sorry I can't pay for you to come back. But the solar hot water panel,' I said (it was already on site, lying against the bank), 'can I get that back to you? I can't pay for that yet, either.'

'Our family went through a difficult time once,' Quentin said. 'I understand what it's like. How about I come over one day when I visit my dad in Palmerston. I'll hook up the kitchen sink and bathroom for you. And keep the solar panel there. You don't have to pay me till you can. I've got a job starting as foreman for a company. I don't need the money just now.'

'That would be amazing. Thank you.'

'It won't be for a while,' he said. 'We've got a new baby and the new job. When I can, I'll get there.'

Upstairs, I cut the batts to shape and Sam fitted them between the joists. The house was quiet, the wind had dropped.

'Look outside,' said Sam.

First there were a few flakes, and then the air was dizzy with snow. We climbed downstairs and stood at the window. You couldn't see the mountains or the willows across the paddock for the swirling flakes. The sky was heavy with grey, snow-bellied clouds. I went outside for another boxful of willow logs for the fire. Snow stung my cheeks and hands. The air was icy to breathe. The precariousness of a life without warmth.

Sam was scheduled to leave in the middle of May. His six months of working on my house was up, and he and Hana had a family holiday booked. I missed the last four tumultuous days working on the house together as it was Bridget's graduation at Massey for her Master's degree. She'd come newly widowed to help with my straw walls and I would be there for her at her ceremony.

Sam left for Queenstown the night before I drove back to the Ida Valley. When I'd headed away to the ceremony in Palmerston North, the inside of the house was still a building site. The scaffolds were set up in the sitting room for putting in the high batts, the drop saw was set up in the hall, there were ladders and tools and mud all over the floor.

'I worked right till late,' Sam called me to say, 'but I'm sorry, I didn't get time to clean up anything or put the scaffolds away.'

'That's ok. I know you were doing all you could. Thank you, Sam. For everything.'

'It's been great,' he said. 'See you on the next building site. And enjoy your beautiful house.'

When I drove in the dark over Black's Hill and up the long straights to the village, I tried to stay positive about what was ahead of me. It was late at night and I was going to a building site to live. No more Sam. No more team. I'd given up the rent on the neighbouring house, so my unfinished house was home now. I had one plug outside for electricity, no plumbing, no furniture, and damp mud walls. I wondered where I would put a mattress for sleeping.

The moon was a sliver in the sky and the stars were out by their thousands. I walked up to the darkened house, opened the door and shone the torch in. Ohhh Sam. I stood there a moment taking it in. Gone the scaffolding, the tools, the ladders and planks. The big kitchen/living room was swept clean and empty, except for a couch pulled up in front of the fireplace. Sam had left me a home to move into.

I lit the fire with pinecones and willow twigs, then lit candles and placed them on the windowsills. They flickered against the dark windows and shone back doubled. The walls – ah, the finality of that word – the walls had a presence of their own, as if they were ancient and their textures spoke of histories I had no knowledge of. Something deeper than sand and earth. They were rock, tree, bone. The walls watching me as well, like guardians.

I carried the mattress that was propped in the hall and placed it down by the fire. I made the mattress up with sheets and duvet from my car. And then I sat on the couch in the warmth of the fire, and looked around me in wonder.

Home.

Now that I was shifted in, winter began in earnest. The tap outside, my only water supply, sometimes froze until mid-afternoon. Obtaining water became more than just lugging the bucket up the slippery, muddy path – 'mud as runny as honey' as Indy described it. It was also a matter of timing, watching the sky for sun on the pipe, making sure to fill the bucket before the pipe froze again.

Buckets made me frugal with water. And collecting water connected me to the past, to those miners who lived in the tents in the gold-mining days just up the road; they, too, out in the snow with cold fingers on the bucket handles.

One morning I stood in the half dark of my unfinished house and looked out as snow fell. It wasn't sideways-blown snow yet, but the flakes were fat and soft as they poured and poured from the sky, falling thickly on the windowsill and on the tops of the fence posts and all over the hard-bitten grass.

I faced into the snow as I walked to the shop, holding my jacket hood on, my gumboots plunking down on the white path. All about me the air was grey.

At the shop Rhonda passed me my mail. 'Have you got plumbing on yet?' she asked.

'No, maybe next week.'

At home, the shifting snow on the roof crunched and rattled like muted gunfire.

The fire was central to my life. With no electricity or oven I could only cook food on the fire. I always had a kettle on, and soup often on the boil. In fact it was two years before I acquired an oven and by then I was well used to making do with wood my sole source of heat and power. The fire kept the house warm, despite no curtains, no ceilings, no floor coverings and snow sometimes half-a-metre deep outside.

A winter shower consisted of heating water on the fire, tipping it into a bucket, carrying it precariously out over snow to the corrugated-iron toilet 'room', stripping off and pouring the bucket of warm water over myself. It reminded me of those days in the hut, when we heated water on the fire for a wash by candlelight.

The mud walls weren't drying in the winter air, even with the fire going all day. We'd been told not to plaster mud inside beyond April, for that very reason, but time had run out and we'd plastered till the middle of May. The morning I found a sprout of barley growing green out of the wet kitchen wall, I walked down to Beckers to ask for the loan of their big diesel blower. With a roaring and a stink of diesel fumes, the blower pumped heat onto the walls and the grey mud began to turn a creamy colour as it dried. With my bedroom walls dry, I scrubbed the spattered mud from the floor and brought my queen-size bed over from Queenstown. Finally I had a bedroom.

I'd also brought back an old enamel candlestick holder from England, and that night I carried it in front of me to light my way to my room. I was struck by the poignant thought that some other hands had held it out in front on the way to their bed.

A month later, Quentin called in to do the plumbing, I went to the kitchen tap and it took only a small movement of my wrist to bring forth water. Seamlessly I moved over from tent dweller, house camper, to an ordinary person who washed dishes in the sink and showered inside. I want the memories of snow and frozen pipes to keep me respectful of water. And also to remind me of the kindness of one person to another to get things done.

CHAPTER 20

Everything is Art

Falling through the roof is not the cleverest start to summer 2014, not with metres of mud to make and plaster onto strawbale walls. Three of my children and their partners, Hana and Sam, Rory and Bailey, and Nick and Bex, had come together for ten days of Central Otago skies. And how fortuitous that was for me, when I stepped backwards, unthinking, through the trapdoor in the loft. I crunched my ribs and tore my knee on the first fall, and then, upside down, fell the rest of the way from the ceiling into the arms of my son Nick.

Nick and Bex drove me to hospital. I hugged my chest, numb with shock. My tongue was so clumsy when I tried to speak, the doctor thought I must have hit my head as well.

'Do you know what day it is?' he asked. A question I have to think about before answering even on a good day.

'It's the 27th of December,' I said, still holding onto my chest. 'Saturday.' I could have said Twosday – one step forward and a lot more than two steps back. Oh, a lapse of concentration with such frustrating and painful consequences.

Back in the 1940s, the Reverend Stalky of Masterton had written in my father's autograph book, 'Rain is wet, hail is worse. Welcome what you are sent.' There could have been much more serious outcomes from the fall. Instead, even in the hospital emergency room, I was grateful for what I was sent: a son in the right place and only broken bones, not something much worse.

To think, last summer when I was building the house with Sam, I'd spent months climbing up and down ladders and walking across beams. I'd only once had a fall, and that's because I was slightly showing off. Now that I lived in the house and the major building of it was over, I'd forgotten words that Brian and Sam had coached me with, words like 'carefully' and 'awareness'. Words I would do well to remember.

I'd fallen at the end of a long day at the concrete mixer making the new batch of mud. Rory and Bailey had worked with me. One of us sifted the clay, one carried the buckets of sand and straw, and one fed the concrete mixer, pouring each creamy-textured mix into the old bath. It was bright out there in the warm sun, and three people made the job fun. In the gardens, flowers blazed: purple and blue lupins and cornflowers, red poppies, scarlet hollyhocks, and the silvery, feathered heads of toetoe and native grasses.

My best memories of mud-making are always of the people who helped make it – that first frenzy with Rory and Brian on the clay; later on Declan and I out there talking about the life of artists; the women who came to help me: Antonia and Angela and Nicole; and Rory and I working late into the night by torchlight to get mud down.

The times I made it myself were some of the lowest points of building. It was then I most missed another's strength. I missed the camaraderie of talking that helped labour go swiftly. On my own, doing the repetitive task of shaking the banana box full of clay backwards and forwards (and somehow it was often frustratingly windy when I was doing it), I'd reflect on things I couldn't influence anymore. I'd think of things I could have said to my first husband, Liam, 30 years ago when I was young and knew nothing of marriage. I'd pull regrets up in my head, words I'd said, which I ought not to have said. How things could have turned out then.

We desire a truthful life, yet what does that ask us to abandon? How to endure that?

Was it the sifting that stimulated those memories, the guilt, the longing for connection? Was it because there were so many parts to making the mud – not just the sifting, but the heaving up of the buckets of clay and the buckets of sand, each time needing strength and fortitude that was fast running out? But to make mud with others, that was simply pleasure. Talking time, laughing time, and not thinking time. And I especially appreciated it when someone else helped lift the buckets.

The mud we'd made in the bath and drums that Christmas of 2013 turned sleek and ready under the tarpaulins shading it from summer sun. But another few days and it would be ruined. Despite me being injured and unable to walk, we *had* to get on with plastering. The west wall needed another protective coat, and the front of the house was still bare straw – tempting to nesting birds and runaway calves. The family and Brian worked together while I did what I could, standing upright in one place with a crutch. Handful by handful we rubbed the silkiness of the mud into the straw, transforming the front wall from golden textured strands compressed and tied together to a sculptured, hand-smoothed wall of mud.

Once the family had returned to their lives in Queenstown and Wellington and Auckland, I was alone in the countryside, still unable to walk or drive. How precious our bodies are. How precious our health and independence. I lay in bed and looked out at the garden, unwatered and turning wild. I thought about all the mud I wanted to make and plaster while it was summer and still warm, and how that wasn't going to happen now, the house inside unfinished for another year. I thought how I couldn't even walk 10 feet, let alone be able to walk to the shop six houses down the road for supplies.

When you're injured or sick or alone, that's when you realise the extent to which the availability of convenient travel, made possible by fossil fuels, has split our families apart, around our own country and across the world. You recognise how loneliness is born out of this. How, and not so long ago, families stayed in the area they were born, always there.

Friends and people in my adopted village stepped in and made sure I received food and coffee and prescriptions. I so appreciated it. When you have no independence, community is precious.

One day, resting on the couch with my injured knee raised on a pillow, I looked outside to the swirling willows by the Ida. Green grass, a muddied, ruffled pond. No other sound in the house. I stared out at rocks on Blackstone Hill. There wouldn't ever be again that time of Sam and I building with the team. The house was liveable. I'd chosen this patch of countryside in New Zealand to stay. Now I just had to get on with things. This was it.

Where do you go from there? It isn't just happy ever after. The 'torment of self' as Hermann Hesse's *Siddhartha* says, that still has to be dealt with.

I looked up and around at my walls, at the handprints in the mud. The fact I wasn't cut off from the earth, but encompassed by earth, helped. I followed the pattern of handprints in the mud. The memory of those who had come and shared their time and skills gave me comfort. The ridges in the mud recalled their names. Yet here I was, propped on a couch. The sense of flatness remained.

Sometimes the various lives I'd left behind felt as if they were just below the surface of this new life. My old life, with the sheen of sea at dawn, or the beech trees and rocks in the mist, was going on regardless and I wasn't there, yet I *was*. And in this life where I lived now, with frost coming unexpectedly on the poppies and the mountains scarlet in the evening, I was also here, and not here.

What stays is everything that doesn't think: the tussock grass, the pines with their serrated profiles, the gullies on Mt Ida in the afternoon light, long clouds lit along their edges. Yet I toss and turn in my mind in those other lives: the iron hut on the steep hillside, two glasses of red wine on a grey formica table and out the window flanks of grass, the fallen beech, the sea.

No wonder sometimes it's hard to get a bearing. For instance, how do I account for the baby I held who became strong enough to toddle, to leap off sandhills, to shift away? It's as if all we love is a river streaming away from us, memories the rounded, clinking boulders that shift beneath our feet. And our job is to hold on to where we are. *To be here.*

All day flocks of sheep and their lambs were driven up the road and back again, like reruns of old movies. Now and again Barry yelled at a dog, and the thousand-fold of hooves on the road sounded like the shushed clattering of stones down a scree slope. I watched the sheep from my window, sometimes a tourist's car surging behind them.

'I can't stand drivers dribbling along at 10 kilometres,' Barry had told me. Me being one of those drivers. 'If you come into a flock of sheep, keep the pressure on them. They'll always move sideways. It's very hard to run over a sheep.'

'What about a speeding driver?'

'I might throw something at them,' Barry said. 'Bloody hoons. Or I'll point the truck at them to slow them down.'

The feeling of loss and loneliness lingered. I took myself outside one lunchtime and sat in the rocking chair in the heat of the sun. *I am so lonely, I am so unsuitable, I am so …* I sat there feeling empty, my arms a heavy weight on the chair arms, my feet heavy on the planks. A gnawing inside as if I hadn't eaten for days. There was nothing I felt able to do. The loss of want. The loss of desire. The loss of hope. I tipped my head back, squeezed my eyes shut.

'Oh, go and get a book,' I said out loud. 'At least read something!' I made myself stand up and go inside. I picked up *Siddhartha* again, brought it out to the sun. I read a few pages, and came across a sentence so rhythmic and melodic and evocative that I had to get a pen and write it down in my journal.

I kept reading and found another passage, and I was overcome then with such a love for words that I was refilled with an energy and equilibrium. Not full of self-pity, unplugged and pale of spirit, but jounced by a desire for creativity; my own desire that had nothing to do with anyone or anything else, but that hard, deep drive to create.

'The simplest thing is, when you are being you, there's no effort. All the weight's removed,' Graeme Male had said to me once. And I forget that at my peril. To write. To create. This is my wellspring.

When I woke each morning I took an exploratory deep breath to check out my ribs, those tenuous parameters of my lungs. I tried not to shift my right knee. But gradually the lengths I could walk with my crutches increased. I could step down from the verandah and over to my garden, where golden rye grass and white yarrow prevailed amongst the poppies. One day a triumph to reach the cafe and order a coffee. Another day, a raggedy lurch along the footpath all the way to the general store.

'I'm rusting up,' I told my doctor, Verne Smith, at my check-up in early February. 'And there's so much to be done on the house.'

'You can begin weight bearing,' he said. 'Exercise will help rebuild the muscles.'

That was good. More than good. I had mud to make.

'Can I carry buckets of mud?'

'Yes,' he said, 'and cycling will be good for your knee.'

When I was able to walk more freely, I clambered down a shingly cliff late one afternoon to the Manuherikia River. It was almost sunset. Brian stood in the shallows and cast and cast his line. I sat on a grey river stone and watched the sky begin to blaze over the cliffs. The fishing line moved back and forth in a fluid curving S to lie on the water amongst the hatched mayflies and the froth from a small stream entering the main flow.

There was a trout but it didn't bite. Its head rose up, and then the sharp arrow of its tail as it dived to feed; a small shark of a trout in a darkening pool.

We walked back, carefully criss-crossing the river over slippery boulders to the car. No fish but a sight of fish, and tangerine and pink clouds in the western sky.

The Manuherikia flows from up the valley, rising between the St Bathans and Hawkdun ranges. We'd followed it once before, up a gorge of deep pools and small runs to the Falls Dam, a lake flattening out into a tussocked high plateau beneath the Hawkduns. There, on Fiddler's Flat, are ruins of cottages, chimneys like raised entranceways to other skies.

Gold came out of the Manuherikia, and camps of miners made brief townships along its banks and inland terraces. Today gold is still mined in Central Otago, in alluvial, open pit and underground mines near Omakau, Moa Creek, Earnscleugh and Kyeburn.

Did the Ida Burn ever carry gold? I bought an old gold pan the same week I bought the land. With a historic gold mine further up, the Golden Progress Mine, and a new one further down the Ida, I thought maybe there would be flecks to harvest in my own stretch of water. So far no luck.

Instead the Ida Burn has given me sand. The same major flood that created a seven-foot deep swimming hole, which lasted all the first summer, carried loads of gravel and sand across my paddocks, miraculously dumping them in sorted piles and drifts as if an excavator and sifter had been at work.

When I walked down to see what the new grey shapes were across the paddock, I found a pile of fine river sand, tonnes of it, a rich deep lode near the willows.

'Where there is no pit sand, we must use the kinds washed up by rivers or by the sea,' Vitruvius wrote, over 2000 years ago, '... and other problems we must solve in similar ways'. Harvesting the sand proved to be a pleasurable exercise: hours of walking in the sun and through the stalky grass to carry buckets of sand to the trailer.

To plaster a house with mud is one joy; to make plaster out of the sand given freely and unexpectedly by a river, is another.

Carrying the buckets through the grass gave me a chance to look around at what was growing. A few months back, a medical herbalist, Isla Burgess, had visited me and taken me on a walk through my paddocks identifying the plants. Now I said the names to myself as I swished through the knee-deep grasses: here, the long-seeded timothy and cocksfoot, here the shimmery wafts of Yorkshire fog grass, yellow-flowered hawkweed, and red clover, yellow dock, Californian stinkweed, sheep sorrel, mouse-eared chickweed, St John's wort, yarrow and mallow. Not just grass and weeds, but each plant useful and named. In the stream, watercress, and above it the electric blue of dragonflies.

The next batch of mud I made with the sand, I used to plaster the first framed, interior wall – a gib wall covered in old carpet and now the recipient of mud. Jazz playing on the stereo, the house warm, and my first attempt at plastering onto the gib looked good. The gib gave a straightness and evenness to the plastering that was harder to achieve over straw. I smoothed the mud out with a trowel, working one section at a time.

The hardest task, with my sore ribs, was bending over the bath outside to lift handfuls of the cold and gritty mud into the bucket, then carrying the heavy weight of it around the house, up the steps and through the door. After four days of carrying sand and making mud, I felt my knee straighten and I began to breathe more easily. The buckets of sand, and then the buckets of mud, felt good to carry.

While I plastered the hall, Graeme worked on a stone wall he was building round the fire. Once an artist who painted with oils, he now found his attraction to art lay in stone. It was not so much that he had walked away from painting, but that '*Everything* I do is art,' he'd told me. He was making art building my fireplace. I was making art smoothing the mud in a pleasing way across the wall. We worked companionably together with music playing and the swooshing of our trowels. I thought of Thoreau writing, 'To maintain one's self on this earth is not a hardship but a pastime, if we will live simply and wisely.'

When I finished my wall I washed my hands and arms and buckets and picked up a small pointing trowel. Here was a chance to learn another skill.

Graeme showed me how to scrape and brush the mortar to reveal the beauty and shape of the stones. Time seemed to slow as I worked. Each stroke with the trowel took care, and so my mind became focussed. One stone, and another stone. A sweep with the brush to reveal progress.

Graeme packed up at five and said I'd learnt enough to carry on and finish the job. He'd mortared this layer of stones in yesterday, and the mortar, after this many hours, was firm enough to scrape yet soft enough to be biddable. Leave it another day and the mortar would be like scraping stone itself.

As the sun came in the corner window and cement dust hovered in the air, I scraped and guided a knife and trowel until all the roughened mortar was made smooth, like water again, flowing between the joints and crevices of rocks.

I remembered the day we all went to the river together to look for stones. Brian's son, Andre Lopez-Turner, was over from London, and I had two wwoofers (Willing Workers on Organic Farms) from California, RJ Roush and Natalie Okun, who had come to work on a strawbale house. We'd set off in our own directions across the rocks, looking for flat-faced stones or ones with interesting colours or shapes and textures. The sun shone and all we could hear was the river; a soft sound of rapids near us from one small river, the Dunstan, and a louder clattering and rattling sound of the Manuherikia. Beside us it swirled into a pool deep enough, though too cold, for swimming.

RJ emerged from the water with a glistening coppery boulder in his arms. Andre and Graeme walked up the riverbank with rocks in their arms. Natalie and

I fossicked along the water's edge. We shared a picnic of Anzac biscuits and pears with bottles of water, taking in the sun and the sound of the water.

In the afternoon, once we'd watched the video Declan had made of Sven plastering with mud, RJ lifted buckets of mud up the ladder. Time to tackle the wall in the loft – RJ and Natalie's first plastering. I showed them how to twist the straw to fill holes, the way Pat had taught me, and how to rub the mud firmly into the straw, without lifting the hand off, the way Sven had shown me. There we were, crouched on the floor in the tightest corner of the house, RJ cross-legged and bare feet, Natalie in a summer dress, each with our bucket of mud. Handful by handful we rubbed the mud into the straw.

We worked till eight at night, the tarpaulins on the floor covered in mud and straw, and our feet and clothes and arms and even faces muddy. We lifted the buckets down and washed them, folded the tarpaulin, swept the floor of straw, and posed for photos all muddied in front of the fire, our arms around each other.

Graeme had finished another layer of stones and mortar and lay back on the couch, as exhausted yet replete as we were. The bold design of the fire surround had come from Graeme and RJ and Natalie. I'd given them full rein to come up with a design. Left to myself I would have opted for a small, safe, minimum fire surround. They had the rocks stretching metres from the fire in two directions, with a sculptured seat and a place for wood.

'I didn't know I could do this in life,' Natalie said. 'Make up a design, and build it for myself for a house.'

I like to think of them going back to America and London with the memories of rocks and sand they carried and mud they made, and a fireplace and a plastered wall that emerged from their own ideas and work. And to know that it is possible to wrest their own shelter in such a way: out of inspiration and imagination, and through simple work with their hands.

I sat at the table with my laptop to write. Sorting words, Brian said, is like choosing stones, trying them out for placement, setting some aside, discarding some, placing others with care in the right place, to make something of craft and beauty that will last. Like the stone wall around my fire.

CHAPTER 21

A *Compagnon* in the Village

'Bonjour,' I said to Lisa Fridd, serving at the counter when I went into the shop for my mail.

'You're the second person speaking French this morning,' she said. 'Brian was in here a few minutes ago.'

There are 29 people who live in the village, some of them part-time or holiday owners, and for a while, a young Frenchman became the thirtieth. Charly Le Bonté had contacted me through the wwoofer website, said he was a joiner and would like to come and help me on my house. A joiner. How could I say no? I picked him up in Queenstown, a young man, mid-twenties, tall, bearded and quiet.

I knew little of his background then, nor the sustained training he had had in France and the fine work he was capable of. What I required was a ceiling in my bedroom out of the leftover macrocarpa panelling in the shed, a bay windowseat out of leftovers, and a front door.

Charly assessed each job. He asked me about the tools I had.

'Do you have a pin gun?'

'Um, no.'

'Do you have a good drill?'

'No.'

'A planer?'

'No.'

Sam had lent me quite a few tools when I picked up Charly, and I proudly owned a drop saw, bought from a man who was leaving the country.

'This is good,' said Charly, looking at the drop saw.

'Will you be able to do the jobs?' I asked him.

'Yes,' he nodded. 'Is possible.'

My friend Steve Aldridge arrived with a boot load of power tools. 'Borrow

At last a front door, thanks to Graeme and Charly.

anything you want,' he said, and Charly stood at the open boot choosing what he needed.

Graeme came down with his drill and stayed to work. His mission: to help get the door in. For two years my entranceway had been boarded up with plywood. Down it came, and for the first time, sunlight brightened the hallway.

On the second day I learnt Charly liked to paint.

'I always like to be doing something,' he said. 'I am used to this, to work all the time.'

I gave him my acrylics from art classes, and heavy paper, and that night he sat at the table sketching his girlfriend back in France.

Each day Charly and I worked, making and plastering mud, and at night Graeme came, or Brian, to share meals Charly had helped cook. The wine was wrapped in a teatowel and placed in the fridge until dinner. Our school-time French was brought out for a good run.

Charly was surprised we didn't say a blessing to each other before meals. 'In France, we don't eat till everyone is seated. Usually we wait for my grandmother who is cooking. When she sits we all say *Bon appétit* to each other, and then we eat,' he said.

He wondered also about our workplace greeting. 'Places I've worked in New Zealand, people might say hello, but in France, every morning when you arrive on site, you shake hands with each person and say *Bonjour*. Because we are a team,' he said.

Months later, when I drove over to Queenstown to help Sam out on the building site, I walked into the framed-up house and searched out Charly, who was now working for my family.

'*Bonjour* Charly' I called.

'*Bonjour* Jillian,' he called back with a big grin. But I forgot to shake his hand.

Sam set Charly and I the task of fixing all the bracing from the triboard walls into the concrete pad. We worked room by room together, me struggling with the electric drill until Charly showed me again how to hold it straight.

We worked together, too, on Graze, the cafe/restaurant Hana, Sam and his dad Dennis were building in Lake Hayes Estate. In the last frantic week, Rory came down from Auckland, and daughter Evie, on a university break, from Wellington to help. It was like the strawbale build all over again, two generations of family working side by side. We sat together in the new courtyard for smoko, me happy with my coffee just looking at them all. Phoenix and Indy clambered over their big Uncle Rory. Sonny was tucked up in the pushchair beside me, eating broccoli. It was good to have Evie on a work site with us (she'd helped Dennis with concreting all morning). And I pictured Merrin, with her shining eyes, sitting there, too, with her sisters.

Sam and Hana set up the company Deavoll Construction after he'd finished our build. I still get to wear my toolbelt there and have smoko with the men. After dinner, if the deadline is tight, I'll go back to the building site with Sam and carry on.

One evening both of us were up on the roof at sunset. I did my usual job of setting out bracing, clambering over and under the roof trusses, agile as a cat now and not scared of heights. Sam became less of the site boss he was during the day and more like the teacher he was in our early days of building together. He climbed over to where I was working.

'Remember not to put bracings where you don't need to,' he said. 'See, there's a wall under this section of the ceiling.'

'Ok,' I said.

'I really appreciate you being here to help,' he said. 'It makes a big difference.'

However many hours in the day he worked, Sam still found energy to encourage me and respect what I did. Even if the only tool I remembered how to use was my favourite, the drop saw.

Charly had been trained for eight years as a joiner in France, as part of an association with a history stretching back to medieval times. Charly was a *Compagnon*, from the Association Ouvrière des Compagnons du Devoir. We leaned over the bench together one night looking on his laptop at pictures of furniture he'd built as part of his training. This Association arose when the first cathedrals had been built, and master craftsmen had worked beside young apprentices. The system of teaching continues, the old share their knowledge and skills with the young. Charly's oldest teacher was 86 years old and taught him to make windows for a castle. Once accepted into the Association, it is for life.

'It's like a marriage,' said Charly. 'You are always there for each other and you are always available to teach the younger ones.'

After a year of training, where all the young men live together in one house, and share it with the older craftsmen who come to help them in the weekends, some are chosen to go on the Tour de France. Not the bike race, but a lifestyle of travelling and living in different parts of the country, working with different craftsmen. Charly travelled and worked for five years. At the end, from the 100 young men who first began training together, and the 10 who were selected to travel for five years, only one was chosen to become a *Compagnon*, Charly.

'As part of our training, we learn to live with certain virtues,' Charly said. 'Patience, fidelity, honesty, fraternity, discipline, courage, bravery, generosity. It's good. Whenever you strike a hard time in life or with someone, you stop, think, remember the virtues, and all is ok. These are what you live by if you accept to be a *Compagnon*. And the older men are there to help you in your life. There is always someone next to you.'

One day another Frenchman turned up in the village to visit Brian. David

146

Charly's ceiling of macrocarpa and pallet wood.

Fauquemberg, a writer, was in New Zealand on a six-month fellowship at Randall Cottage in Wellington. He told Brian about one of his friends, who was a *Compagnon* in France.

'There's another *Compagnon* just down the street,' Brian said, and brought the surprised David over to meet Charly. I was sleeping after working a nightshift and didn't get to meet David then.

In the weeks Charly had stayed with me, I'd taught him how to make mud and to plaster the walls. In return, Charly had created a work of art for me on my bedroom ceiling.

I hadn't enough long pieces of macrocarpa left to finish the ceiling.

'What about using pieces of old pallet wood?' Graeme had suggested. I had pallets out the back holding the tarpaulin down over my clay supply. The wood was weathered grey, pitted with old nail holes.

'Is possible,' Charly had said. 'Jillian, you draw a design.'

I looked around the room. In a jug stood flax flowers I'd made as table decorations for Hana and Sam's wedding eight years before.

'How about a woven pattern?' I said. 'For me it will mean the weaving together of family and friends.'

Charly designed the pattern on his computer, cut the macrocarpa and pallet wood on the front deck and assembled and glued the design in front of the fire on a freezing cold afternoon. Just like the slaked lime I made later, I love to show the ceiling to visitors.

I'd been disappointed not to meet David Fauquemberg when he visited my house. I met him instead at a house concert in Wanaka a week later. He was talking in a group of people when I was introduced.

'Hi David,' I said. 'It's nice to meet you finally. Did you see my bedroom ceiling?'

That took some explaining to the others, about old pallet wood, joinery and a skilled *Compagnon*.

My house had straw walls filled in and mud plastered over top, even some ceilings in place. Outside, the ubiquitous silver tarpaulins sheathed portions of the house. They kept wind-driven rain and summer sleet from the mud. But the wind was taking its toll – there were rips and holes where water could get in. Sam was too busy with his growing family and construction business to come over from Queenstown to help. It was up to me to finish the house. What the walls needed for protection, instead of tarpaulins, was lime.

PART FOUR

LIME

Why not consider a house animate? Why not relate to it as a living being? Why not honour a house with a name and greet it with common decency and good manners.

– CHARLES GOODRICH, *THE PRACTICE OF HOME: BIOGRAPHY OF A HOUSE*, 2004

CHAPTER 22

A White Substance on a Spade

A long way into the building project I discovered a book a woman wrote about building her mudbrick cottage in 1941 in the Bay of Islands, New Zealand. Charlotte Larkin was 60 when she began to build herself a home. Her husband was dead; her two sons were away at war. She wanted to do something that would inspire the young New Zealand men who would return.

She herself was at a turning point in her life. 'Physically, mentally, financially, I had been under a severe strain ... I was now homeless, but free. Free to roam where I liked. But where?' She sat in an old deck chair and let her mind drift.

'A home, that is what a man will need: a home built at a minimum cost; a home that will inspire him and raise his spirits through creative work ... I knew I must prove it possible, although I had little money, little strength, and no knowledge of building.'

Charlotte's words echoed my own sentiments when I had started the house project. On the one hand, belief that it is possible, and not only that, belief that it is better for society for people to have warm and creative home-made homes. But on the other hand, all the questions and doubts, the lack of knowledge and resources, and the hard work ahead.

And there was hard work ahead. Two walls of the house were still covered in tarpaulins. The whole house needed two coats of lime plaster and five coats of lime wash. And for all of this I needed slaked lime (burnt lime soaked in water to become putty).

Lime for slaking is burnt at 1000°C. When it's added to water, the lime immediately boils, and extreme care needs to be taken. The prospect of slaking the lime daunted me. Where would I purchase the lime and how would I slake it, and in what?

My journal was full of lists and lines to myself: *I need to make the plaster. I need to know how. I need the lime here soaking. I need drums. I need lime. I need money for the lime. I need to know how much lime. I need an experienced plasterer to put it on. I need the colour to go into the plaster. I need scaffolding. I need big tarpaulins and someone to help put them up. I need the plastering done before the weather gets too hot, and before the winter comes …*

It was already late October, the poppies a blaze of red amongst the blue cornflowers and lupins, the mountains snow-free and the sky a blue canvas for white clouds. The paddocks of lucerne across the road rippled silvery in the wind. And the lambs, which had just a few weeks ago run up and down the fence lines in tribes of skinny, wrinkled creatures, were now woolly and plump, grazing beside their mothers.

The lime plaster needed to be put on before the summer sun got too harsh. And not only that, when I looked at my calendar, I realised I was running out of time to finish the outside of the house before my code compliance certificate expired in March. Before I could plaster, though, I needed *months* in which to slake the lime.

Burnt lime needs a minimum of three months to soak in water and become workable. Traditional Japanese plasterers will soak the lime for their child's house when the child is born. Twenty years is a good amount of time to slake lime. I only had just over three months.

Because of lack of knowledge and fear, I'd kept putting off the task of slaking the lime. No Sam to check up on me and make lists at night and deal with contractors in the morning, the job completed by afternoon. Everything planned for, organised and carried out to a schedule when Sam and I were building together.

Left to my own devices, what was too hard was avoided. Besides, I was working one or two shifts each week as a nurse aid at the hospital in Ranfurly, 20 minutes away in one direction, paying Sam back with labour a day or two on his building site in Queenstown two hours in the other direction, and working on my laptop at home in between times. How could I fit lime in? The fact there was a deadline pushed it right up my list of priorities.

And I found (like Charlotte Larkin had), that when I committed to a course of action, advice, materials and helpers arrived. Commitment to action was the important step.

Often, when you don't know what to do or how to start, all it takes to solve problems is to ask questions. Chris Cox reminded me I could get the lime in Dunback, and gave me the name of a plasterer skilled in historic buildings. The plasterer told me how many sacks of lime to get (15–16; I got 18 for good measure). Chris told me to slake the lime in an old bath. And Warehouse plastic rubbish bins.

'Not plastic bins,' the plasterer said, 'they'll melt. Use steel drums.'

'But not steel drums,' another plasterer told me, 'they'll corrode. Use plastic.'

I thought I would use everything, and find out myself what worked. But where to get them? The day I decided I had to get the lime and find the drums and bath and slake the lime and get it done that very week to be ready in time, I walked down to the shop for my mail. I waited behind a farmer, Richard Anderson, who was getting his mail.

'I found a sheep drowned in that old bath lying in my paddock,' he said to Lisa at the counter.

'Excuse me,' I said. 'Do you want to sell that bath? I need one for making lime.'

'You can have the bath,' he said. 'I'll drop it off today.' And he did.

One down. In the afternoon Brian came by with his trailer hooked on the car. We drove to Ranfurly and asked questions at the garage and at the rubbish dump. We were directed from place to place till eventually we found six steel drums and two plastic ones. By day's end I'd rung Taylors at Dunback and ordered the sacks of lime, booked in the plasterer and assembled most of the drums. From a quest I had shied from, I now knew much more about what to do. I even had the recipe for lime plaster:

Into the concrete mixer: one-part slaked lime, four-parts sand, water to mix.

No one, however, could give me a recipe for slaking the lime. *Just keep adding it to water, and mix until it's stiff. Carefully,* was the advice I was given.

'And don't do it inside,' Chris told me when I called in on the way to Dunback. 'I set up a bath, tipped in a sack of lime and hosed it from a distance to get water on it. The steam that comes up is dramatic. You do know,' he added, 'that you don't have to buy burnt lime? You can get sacks of pre-slaked lime and add them to water. It's much easier.'

'But I'm looking forward to doing it the traditional way,' I said. 'I read that lime putty was the most weatherproof lime. I want to use the burnt lime. And besides, the sacks are all ordered and especially bagged for me.'

'It's a terrible job,' Chris said. And he was over six foot and strong. 'I never want to do it again.'

How right he was.

But that day, I was excited to drive up to the lime kilns in the hills behind Dunback, an hour away over the Pigroot, to see where the lime came from, to bring a trailer-load of sacks home, and finally to begin slaking.

I wasn't on my own for the beginning of this task. Declan had come to the valley to make a short film of Brian fly-fishing. He was also interested to have a go at the lime process. Nothing better than having two people when it comes to taking on a new skill. It was a bright-sky day, the sun shining on the flaxes and tussocks. On Rough Ridge the lambs called out with their high-pitched baby baaas.

Earlier in the morning I'd walked down to the shop for the paper. There are six houses between my place and the old general store, and each front garden was ablaze with spring flowers – irises, daffodils, japonica, wisteria. The air was sweet with the fragrance of *Viburnum davidii*, which was in clustery bloom in each front yard. The wild pink flush of flowers in Brian's crabapple tree had faded but the lilacs along the street were rich with petals and scent. Up the valley, on Blacks Hill, in the rocky paddocks and along the road side, the wild thyme was in full purple bloom, the fragrance in the air there more bitter and aromatic, with a hint of mandarin.

In my backyard, the magician and I stood over the first steel drum half-filled with water.

'You tip, I'll stir,' he said, holding an upended shovel. I had overalls on and rubber gloves and Brian's chainsawing goggles. I tipped in the first small shower of powder. The lime boiled the water so furiously, the 44-gallon drum began to rock. This stuff really did pack a punch.

Gradually I tilted the sack and tipped in the white powder. Steam came up like thick smoke. Once it cleared, Declan stirred with the shovel. It was a slow, pains-taking method to get enough lime, almost the whole 25-kilogram sack, safely into the water to thicken it to a stiff putty. Every now and then we peered into the drum. The lime steamed and bubbled as if this was a cauldron and we the sorcerers.

I wished Declan was staying to help with the sorcery, instead of heading out to fish.

'You know, fly-fishing and being a magician are not that different,' Declan had told me.

'And nor is poetry and magic,' Brian had said. 'Or poetry and fishing.'

'That's right,' Declan said. 'You have to put the time in to practise – and they all depend for success on the skilled presentation of illusions.'

Declan and I started on the second drum of water. Brian pulled up in his car and got out, dressed in fishing waistcoat, rubber boots over his jeans.

'How's everything going?' he asked.

'Good,' I said, 'but don't come too close.'

Declan put down the shovel and lifted his rod and camera from the back of his van.

'Do you guys really want to go fishing instead of making lime?' I asked.

Yes, it looked like it. They drove off, barely concealing their anticipation of pleasure. I stood and looked at the 17 sacks of lime stacked in the carport. Well, it was my house, my 'I can do it myself' idea.

I tipped in lime, waited for the steam to clear, grasped the handle of the shovel and stirred. The goggles I wore steamed up the moment I came close to the drum. Between my blurred vision and the steam rising, I managed to see enough to stir and keep safe. As the lime in the drum got thicker and thicker it took all my strength to move the shovel.

I used a clean shovel to get lime out of the sack. Every few shovelfuls I backed off, pulled off my goggles, and let cool air on my face. I wiped the goggles clear with a rag, put them back on and approached the drum. Immediately they steamed up again. I ignored a splash on my rubber glove, too busy to deal with it, and later found large blisters that took weeks to come right.

By the time I'd finished the second sack, the weather had changed. No more spring. Low grey cloud and a chill wind made a mockery of approaching summer. They say Central Otago can have four seasons in one day, and this felt like winter. There was even a dusting of snow on parts of Blackstone Hill.

After the third 25-kilogram sack I couldn't carry the sacks anymore. I pushed and rolled the fourth sack onto a tarpaulin and dragged it over to the drum. I rolled my shoulders back and forth. Wiped my goggles. Took another deep breath. It began to rain, an icy, stinging rain.

Come on old girl, I said to myself, the way Charlotte Larkin had admonished herself when making mud bricks. *Think of this as the pinnacle of your dream. You're making your own house!*

The night before, Evie had told me her flatmates were watching YouTube videos on alternative houses. 'They want to build one,' she'd said.

I gripped the handle of the shovel. This was the reality. This was what I chose.

And, despite the rain, the stark cold hills, fogged glasses and numb wrists, the lime dissolved and became, at last, another drum of putty.

Three days later I lay on the couch at lunchtime, my arms too sore to lift. I had aloe vera gel smeared over my blistered hand. I'd spent the morning writing, doing housework – anything, in fact, rather than face the remaining seven sacks of burnt lime waiting at the back of the house.

The longer I lay there the more my stomach felt nauseous. I knew there was

Slaking the lime.

only one way to stop feeling sick. *Go and do the work.* It was the thought of stirring thick, bubbling paste in a volcanic drum. It was like working up high on the scary beams again. A terrible job, like Chris Cox said. I never wanted to do it again. Ahh! I pulled on my overalls and goggles. And two pairs of rubber gloves for protection.

The story that affected me most from Larkin's book was the time when her dream nearly ended. All the mud bricks she'd made and the concrete foundations were destroyed in a storm, the very day before bricklaying was to begin.

'For a time I stood, crushed and helpless, just staring at the appalling destruction. The whole hillside seemed to have slipped away. Not a brick, not a tool, not a scrap of foundation was showing. All that showed was a slithering mass of clay, and soil, and shrubs, and crushed flowers ...' Close on 200 tonnes of soil had come down on her building site. She had nothing but her bare hands to clear it with.

How did she carry on? How did she find the strength to start over again? At first it was nature: she saw the slender green shoot of a clematis vine coming up out of the dark soil on the edge of the destruction.

'I, too, will struggle through that earth and also reach the light,' she told herself.

For weeks she bent over, grasped the soil with her hands and flung it out into the small valley. She dug down and down, recovering her tools, discovering the concrete foundation. And letters from her sons away at war helped her keep faith in herself and her task. They simply believed she would do it.

Her hard work I admired, the hours she put in, the way she lived on site in a tent with no power, no running water and barely any tools to make her house. Yet what inspired me more than anything was her tenacity, her strength to keep on with a project and to not lose trust she would succeed.

One thing Charlotte Larkin did, that I also do, is to spend time each morning, before the day's work begins, in meditation. Charlotte sat on a wooden seat she'd made in honour of her soldier sons, her Anzac seat she called it, each morning and night, and asked for guidance.

I have a routine where I ask for blue light. While building my home I would ask for it to bless the working site and each person on it, that they may be safe and skilled and happy; the tools and materials, that they may be safe and arrive on time; and the house made beautiful and strong, a place of creativity and kindness.

I learnt this technique when I was drummer in an all-women's indie pop band. Melita Johnston, guitarist, Fiona Ingram, bass and vocals, and I, drums, were Red Dress. We toured and played for four years, after meeting at music school in Nelson. I was 42 when I went to music school and began in the band. I needed every help then, too, to have confidence, to believe I was good enough to get up and play our own songs in public.

Melita, who had played gigs with David Kilgour of The Clean, taught newbies Fiona and I how to have good energy on stage by a group exercise we did before performing. We'd stand together and imagine blue light coming through our heart chakras in the centre of our chests, surrounding us then going out to fill all the space where we were playing and surrounding each person there as a blessing. We'd then go on stage to perform, as if we had conducted a spell of togetherness and goodwill.

One day, on tour of the West Coast, we had to rush from one gig up to a lunchtime gig at the polytech in Westport. We arrived just in time to set up our gear on stage and begin playing, without our normal routine of blue light. First song, as I began a drum roll on the toms, I threw my drumstick across stage by mistake. And I hadn't put a spare set of sticks by my stool. I kept playing the riff with one stick while Fiona played bass and at the same time used her foot to edge the drumstick closer to me. I hadn't thrown my stick for months, and definitely not at any gigs. We didn't play as well as we wanted, in fact we thought it was a terrible gig, and afterwards, on the road to Greymouth, we talked about what had happened. We remembered we hadn't taken the time to set ourselves up by doing our blue light prayer. We made sure after that we always connected before a performance.

By experiment I sorted out the best method for me for slaking lime. Chris swears by putting a sack of lime in the (outside) bath and then hosing it and stirring it, but I found I didn't have the arm strength to stir a sack of dried lime at once (although the steam is spectacular when you hose it).

Adding burnt lime to water in a Warehouse plastic rubbish bin does not work. I was adding lime and adding water and stirring for a while before I realised the heat from the lime had blown a hole in the bin, the water and lime leaking out as I was putting it in.

Making the lime in the enamel bath and then shovelling it into the rubbish bin for storage works, as the lime putty has cooled down a bit by then. And the rubbish bins have clip-on lids making them easy to store lime in the weather. This was Chris's method.

Slaking lime in high-grade 44-gallon blue plastic drums works well. So does slaking lime in steel drums. I liked the blue plastic ones the best only because they were easier to clean for the lime and are lighter.

The joy of facing a huge writing project, like a novel, is in each sentence. And the joy of slaking the lime was in the creaminess of the lime itself. Drum after drum after drum of such unearthly white substance. It felt like a treasure in my backyard. From this lime would come the protection for my house. There was no need for cement, for processed products, not even for paint.

Lime encapsulated for me what it is to lead a simple life. If you have straw and mud and wood, you can build a house. If you have lime, you can protect it.

Now, any new visitors to my house are invariably greeted with, 'Do you want to see my slaked lime?' I lift back the tarpaulin from the drums, use my old stirring shovel, baked hard with lime, and lift a shovelful of creamy lime up from its protective covering of water.

I'm not sure what other people think when they see it, this white substance on a spade. For me it holds memories of the time of unknowing and procrastination, of steam and stirring and blisters, and now the fact of its existence in my yard, and the treasure to come from it – lime plaster, lime wash; the transformation of the house yet again.

CHAPTER 23

One Wheelbarrow at a Time

It was early morning, grey clouds overhead and a rumbling, hustling wind. The wind was from the south, by the way the toetoe were bending, so probably a cold wind as well. The tarpaulin over the clay pile flapped and strained to be free. The scaffolds were all set up on the Blackstone Hill side of the house, and Sam here for one day to help start me on the lime plastering. We were really going to do it, wind or no wind, rain or no rain.

Once again, it was the seasons running the timetable. March already, 2015. The temperatures dropping, the brief summer and the longer drought over. And the plasterer who was experienced in old techniques, the one who was going to come and do my plastering and train me, had cancelled even though he'd been booked in for months. He was in his 70s and overwhelmed by work. I could understand that.

Worried about the weather, I'd rung Sam to tell him, and we both had the same thought: we'll just do it ourselves. Like Sam had said to me when we first began building, 'There's no such thing as can't on a building site, there's only the job to be done.'

Now, for the first time, after all the months of thinking about it, the lime would be scooped from the drums and put in the concrete mixer, for the first time sand would be added to lime, and for the first time we would know what the plaster mix looked like, and felt like, and acted like to smooth on.

We hosed the west wall, the wall most vulnerable to weather. Sam gathered trowels and buckets and I fluffed around setting up straw bales and planks for a lower scaffold, always that hesitation in me when I had to do something I'd never done before.

'Get the mixer going, Jillian!' Sam called down from the top scaffold. And I had to overcome my fear and ignorance and begin. Like the first sentence of a new story. I flicked the switch on the mixer and used the shovel to lift out lime.

How beautiful it was, like firm whipped cream. I shook it off the shovel into the mixer and added four shovels of sand. Beckers had brought me 5 cubic metres of a fine textured, slightly golden-coloured sand. Chris had told me to also get some sea sand if I could, because that was rich in silicone and would help with the protective coat. But I hadn't found time to get to the coast.

And horsehair, my friend Dwayne Clifton suggested on Facebook. My daughter-in-law's mother, Leslie Davies, who lived in Wales, told me, yes, it's good to use horsehair to stop the cracking. Just sprinkle it in. I didn't have horsehair for those loads and we did get cracking. Later I asked Dave and he sent me some from my horse Rosie, up on his farmlet in Motueka. The hair arrived in time for the interior plastering.

How much water to put in the mix? I didn't know. Or colouring. I threw a scoop of yellow oxide powder into the lime and sand. It turned a buttery yellow. I let the mixer flop over and over for a while, tipped the plaster into the wheelbarrow and then scooped it into buckets for Sam. He hauled them up on a rope to the top of the scaffold. It wasn't the greatest mix. Too pale and too stiff. He could barely smooth the plaster on the wall. But already, with those two buckets, the apex of the house had plaster on it.

Graeme arrived to see how we were doing just as I mixed the second batch. He stood beside me and watched the lime and sand tumble around in the bowl.

'More water,' he said. 'And more lime.' He kept watching. 'Now more water.'

'How can you tell?' I asked. 'Have you made lime plaster before?'

'No, but when I was landscaping the schist around my house I made 700 concrete-mixer loads of cement,' he said. 'I can tell by listening to the mixer. I can tell by eye. Believe me, after 700 loads you get to know what works.'

'That is a lot of physical work,' I said. We stood there watching the grainy mix tumble in the drum. 'How did you keep going?'

'I had my plan, and all my drawings. *Just execute it*, I told myself, *just do it one wheelbarrow at a time*. I couldn't afford a concrete truck or men to help. And when I started each day I got into a rhythm. It's always the mind that is the obstacle,' he said.

'That's for sure.'

'Dreading it. That's the hardest part. The work itself is the easiest part. Ok, put a little bit more water in.'

'And working with someone beside you is especially the easiest part,' I said.

Now the mix changed and flowed around the drum in a mesmerising way. It came cleanly out of the mixer into the wheelbarrow.

'You've got it,' Graeme said. 'Keep it up like that.'

'Yes, this is great,' Sam called later. 'It's going on much more smoothly.'

I had time between making mixes to put some plaster on, myself. I climbed on the straw bales, balancing a heavy hawk-load of plaster and an old steel trowel in my other hand. Finally I got to push my first lime plaster onto the mud wall. The plaster was a sunny, tussocky gold, and textured like grainy cream. But I struggled to have the strength to get the plaster moving across the mud wall. The sharp edges of the trowel dug in and ruined the plaster finish I'd just done. Five minutes into it and my arm was aching. I felt spaced out, almost nauseous, balanced on the plank, not making a good job of it and knowing it with every trowel stroke. I jabbed at the plaster, speared at it, and the precious plaster fell off my hawk and off my trowel and off the wall. I clambered down to get another hawk-load and back up onto my shaky stand. There was more plaster on the ground than there was on the wall.

Sam had his radio on, playing older classics he thought I'd like, and the rain was so far holding off.

'You know, a lot of people wouldn't understand the concept of being happy in your work,' said Sam from the scaffold above me. 'if they work just for money. But to be happy in every moment in what you're doing. Look at us – music on, the lime going up on the wall.'

He was so satisfied, sitting on the scaffold, his innate strength and balance, and the lime going swiftly on. I looked at my choppy little trowel strokes and the marks all over my plaster. My hand was blistered, rubbed raw over the knuckles. My head spun and plaster still fell off the wall with my clumsy efforts. Happy?

The music was good in the bright air, and being back working with Sam was special ('the two battlers,' he'd said as we walked back to work after lunch). And I was happy to see the protective lime going up on the exposed west wall. But happy when you're frustrated?

I had on white overalls like my father always wore at work. I had to trust that trowel by trowel I would start to get better at this.

We worked all day till it was almost dark and chilling down, and we finished one thick coat on that huge west wall. Almost as soon as were done, the wind strengthened and ominous rainclouds threatened from the west, behind Blackstone Hill.

'It's coming,' said Sam. 'Let's get the tarpaulin.' In the wind we fought the silver sheet to screw it to the top boards and down over the scaffolding. Rain

Sam happy in his work plastering lime over mud.

teemed on us, driven against the tarp while we wrangled rocks and logs to pin the tarp to the ground. But the wall was safe.

The next morning Sam left at 5 a.m. to arrive home in time for breakfast with his children. On my own, I made a new mix of lime plaster in the concrete mixer and started again, this time on the long south wall. I'd recently spent three days putting another coat of mud on that south side to straighten it out. I knew that wall pretty well.

The steel trowel still bothered me the way it sliced into the plaster on the wall and knocked it down. I switched to a smaller, wooden floating trowel and found that much easier to use. I pushed plaster up the wall then 'floated' it in circular motions to bring up a pale gold, textured surface. I wasn't dizzy, and I started to get more of a feel for how to push the plaster off the hawk. When I finished the wheelbarrow I reluctantly went back to the mixer to make another load (no one to call out 'Another mix!' to, the way Sam did with me all yesterday.)

At four, Graeme came round to fit a door-jamb inside for me. He stood and looked at my plaster work, with about a quarter of the back wall done.

'Wow,' he said. 'That's beautiful.'

'Really?'

'Yes, it looks great. You've got a natural feel for it. It must be in your genes.'

Just on sunset, the plasterer Ross Miller called in. He'd been working on the historic buildings at Hayes Engineering and I'd asked him to come and check on my plastering. I wanted him to rescue me. I wanted him to come and work for a few days and plaster the high east wall. He looked at my mix in the wheelbarrow.

'This looks good,' he said. 'As long as it isn't so wet that water is seeping out. Are you using the water from on top of the slaked lime?'

'No, just from the tap.'

'Use the slaked water, it's full of minerals.'

He looked at the plastering I'd done that day, and nodded. It was all right. Then he checked the west wall, examining the cracks I was worried about and that had now spread across the whole surface as the plaster dried.

'If you wet the wall, then float the cracks, they should come out. Fill them a bit, if they're deep. And keep the surface rough. Run a yard broom over the wall ready for the next coat, or score the plaster.'

'Do I have to put another coat on?' I asked. 'We put this one on so thick to make up for two coats.'

'You'd want to put two coats on,' he said. 'What you normally do is put two thinner coats on, the scratch coat and a top coat.'

I looked up at the scaffolding to the top level. Sam had said to me, 'You're not to go up to the top. You've already had a fall. You'll have to get someone else to do up there.'

But I didn't want to ask Graeme, who was recovering from an illness, and Ross was busy, and the cracks had to be attended to as soon as possible. *Tomorrow*, he'd said.

Something of the enormity of the task must have registered on my face. All this wall again. And the rest of the long back wall. And all the east wall. And the front of the house. And all of it twice.

'You look worried,' Graeme said.

'That whole wall again,' I said.

'I'll come and help. We'll knock it out. Look at your plastering. It's beautiful.'

'And I might be able to come and do that high east wall,' Ross said. 'Give me a call when you've got the scaffolding set up there.'

The next morning Graeme was there at nine. We hosed the west wall and climbed up the series of ladders with our trowels and buckets of plaster. We were in another world, suspended on a scaffold, in behind the tarpaulin, so that not even sky existed, or sun or trees, but only the wall in front of us.

And the good thing about a high wall and scaffolds is that inch by inch the wall does get covered (we were doing the lightest covering over the thick plaster), and inch by inch the high section is over. Next thing we were off the top layer and on to the sturdier second layer, and then it was time for the cafe.

Brian took a break from writing his book *Boundaries* to join us. We sat outside, Graeme and I in our plaster-encrusted clothes, and the three of us talked about what it is to be community. Brian had lent one of Wendell Berry's books to Graeme and it was having a real effect. Berry is all about the community we live in – the landscape, the creatures and the people we live amongst.

'I had my day planned for today,' Graeme said. 'I had accounting work to do and some online business, but when I saw the look on Jillian's face yesterday – I don't think I've ever seen her look so overwhelmed – I thought about Berry, and how it's more important to help one another,' he said. 'And I'm loving it!'

Brian nodded. He was off to caddy at the New Zealand Open. 'You know, some of those who attend major sporting events, including current and former "stars", come across as pretty pleased with themselves,' he said. 'It helps to have "done well", it opens doors. They've got focus. I just wish more of them would put their hands up, speak out about the most important issues of the day. Few are game or care to piss off sponsors, especially those in the rugby, golf or cricket worlds. They're in a position to do more for what's truly worthwhile, be a bit more courageous.'

'They could read Berry,' Graeme said. 'He clarifies everything I believe in but haven't put into words. I'm grasping the fundamentals, which are immutable, and they're what I've believed since I was a child, and what put me offside with the Auckland I grew up in.'

Philippa brought us out coffee and cheese scones. The rain clouds that had threatened, after a brief shower, set sail for the Mt Ida Range, and beyond.

On Tuesday I plastered another quarter of the south wall, and then it was night shift at the hospital. I still had blisters from the lime on my hands. The nurse on duty gave me gel and I covered my hands in rubber gloves for a night's cleaning work.

The rubber gloves I'd used for plastering were too big and lime mix had fallen in and become trapped around my fingers. Lime is a silent burner. You don't know it's happening till much later. How was I going to hold a trowel the next day? Maybe I shouldn't do anything until my hands healed. But frosts were coming and I needed to finish the plaster. I thought of what Sam had said when I'd asked after his sore arm, how was it after all the plastering?

'It's not good,' he said, 'but I don't think about it. I just have to get on and do things.'

Charlotte Larkin, too, had suffered with painful hands when she was clearing her building site, and went to see a doctor, who had just said, 'What do you expect with the work you are doing? Just don't think about it.'

I set up for plastering again, this time with aloe vera on my hands and wearing medical gloves under kitchen gloves. I shovelled the sand and lime into buckets, as Ross had advised, so that each mix was accurately measured. The mixture flumped over and over in the concrete mixer. I added lime water, scoop by scoop, until the mixture turned from a dry, grainy mix to a soft, almost fluid load that peeled cleanly off the sides of the mixer at each turn. I could tell by eye now how much water needed to go in.

The album *Graceland* played while I floated the first metre of fresh plaster on the wall. As the plaster transformed under the trowel to that golden texture again, I began to feel that happiness that comes when you know you're doing a good job – even if it's just the best you can be doing at the time. I didn't notice my burnt fingers. I climbed up and down my bale ladder with the plaster on the hawk, then I was standing on the ground and eventually I was on my knees to plaster the lowest section of the wall.

I made another mix, shifted the bales along and climbed up with my hawk. I began to feel a rhythm and a fluidity through my shoulder to my trowel, and a strengthening in my arm. The plaster moving smoothly in one motion off the hawk onto the mud. I thought, *I'm a plasterer. I'm a plasterer.*

Like the moment when the plaster changes in the mixer and becomes pliable, like the moment when frothing milk at a cafe and the noise changes in the jug and the foam becomes dense and creamy, *I* had reached that moment. Something in me had changed. Not just the belief I was capable, but a trust in the way my body moved.

I thought about that east wall. I thought, how good would it feel to do the whole wall myself, from the top scaffold down, and then do the front wall, and then do all the walls all over again? How good to be able to look at the house for the rest of my life and know I made every barrow of mix, and plastered the house myself.

CHAPTER 24

Lessons from the Past

The willows along the Ida Burn, cracked from old storms, are great willows, with girths of twenty feet or more. In summer their upstretched branches hold froths of green; in winter they freeze white with hoar frost or give eerie, tracery backdrops to fog and cloud. In high winds their branches break and offer firewood. I make trips back and forth across the paddock with the wheelbarrow in autumn, collecting the cream chunks and rounds to stack on the verandah in the north sun.

One weekend, the grandchildren came to stay. In the morning I wheeled Phoenix in the wheelbarrow, he clutching his yellow truck and a stick, and five-year-old Indy, in her pink gumboots, high-stepping across the long grass, which all summer had browned like tussock and now was flood-flattened and easier to traverse.

A plank of Oregon crosses the stream that comes out of the spring-fed pond. I thought I would have to hold their hands to cross, but first Indy walked over it and then Phoenix wanted his turn, one small gumbooted foot after the other. We checked the pond for ducks, for earlier a group of three had honked across the sky. No ducks, nor pheasants. There is a group of three of those as well, living in the broom here and regally crossing the paddock in search of food.

The neighbours Bruce and Wendy Blakely had their calves in my front paddock. The oldest, a brown calf called Murray, came up to investigate us. His face was wide and flat and swept hairily down to a wet, chocolate brown muzzle, which he pushed in Indy's face and then attempted to lick her. Encounters with Murray, or Mully, as Phoenix says, are the highlight of the morning for the children. Not so much collecting the firewood, which has spiders, according to Indy. The children accompanied me back across the paddock to the promise I'd take them down to look at the lake, which is the circular deep hole the Ida Burn churned out after heavy rain. Back at the house, Hana, with young Sonny, sat reading by the fire in the sun in an old rocking chair.

This was what I dreamed for my house – in the middle of nowhere as my kids first thought, where I wouldn't know anyone, nor how to build a strawbale house or find the straw or the people to help.

Yet it wasn't like that at all, as now they have seen for themselves. This is a house a family helped build, even Indy. Hana tied twine and shifted bales on the strawbale day, Nick and Bex came for straw walls and mud, and Rory was the mud-making man and carpenter. Indy and Phoenix know that Grandma and Dad built the house, and to them it's completely normal. They saw their uncles work here, and their other Nana and Grandad D, and were part of the team sitting on straw bales before the walls began to go up.

They know this house from the empty paddock and scraped building site, when Indy pretended there was a bed in the soil bedroom and lay down on it, and pretended to eat at a table where the dining room would be.

If I am contrite about anything, it's that I didn't foresee how this could be, many more years ago. This situation where my family has free access to me, this time to come and go in a space of wide open skies and mountains at the end of the road.

But regrets have no place in a present moment of getting a wood-laden wheel-barrow to the door, and a safe transport of yellow truck and small boy. Whatever paths we take lead in the end to the life we want, and sometimes those paths just take a longer route because they do, and perhaps that's what was needed at the time.

A few weeks later, I took a journey on a rutted and precarious gravel road, snow piled high in the middle, to find the old stone buildings on the sheep station, Highfield, in Gimmerburn. The autumn snow had mostly gone from the pad-docks and the sky was a pale blue. Who built the early houses, I wanted to know. How were they made?

Highfield is a farm almost opposite where I live in the Ida Valley, but over the other side of Rough Ridge. Here the snow is deeper on the sides of the road, and rocks flare up from the paddocks, small monoliths of schist. No wonder the early pioneers built from stone. There were no trees. They only had rock and earth. The wood for the framing of the roofs and the flooring came from ships, the farmer Pat Dowling told me.

The abandoned homestead at Highfield is a mixture of stone and mud brick; a house that burnt down twice; that is, the roof and wooden parts burnt out twice,

Cottage at Highfield near the supply of rock it was built from.

probably from clothes drying over the fire at night, but the mud walls remained. Thick walls, almost the length of my arm wide.

Pat showed me the kitchen wall of the house. The cupboard was carved into the thickness of the mud wall, so it only needed shelves slotted into it and a cupboard door. I'd never seen kitchen joinery made as part of a mud wall before. One-hundred-and-fifty years hadn't altered their precise, rectangular shape, even without a roof to protect them.

When Pat and Maree bought the farm in 1991, the mud homestead was already beyond repair, the walls half-fallen down into the field and the building without a roof for 90 years. Even so, the mud walls still stood, polished at their bases by sheep rubbing against them, pitted on their tops by the action of rain.

The stone buildings, though, the stables, the meat house and an old cottage, were mostly intact. Pat and his son Luke set about restoring them, taking off the roofs and repairing them, getting in a stonemason to repair missing parts of walls and making sure these beautiful buildings would last another 100 years.

It's not hard to see where these buildings come from. The cottage is only 40 feet or so from the outcrop of rocks that provided schist for its walls. Mud helped provide the mortar, and lime wash a veneer on the outside. The parts of the buildings that have fallen down have gone back into the earth they came from. That's all there was to the buildings. Nothing toxic, nothing wasteful.

All around this district, on road sides and in far paddocks on the big runs, are these buildings, testament to the durability of natural materials, and to the pioneers who came and built thick-walled houses out of the materials to hand. Pioneers starting a new life in a harsh climate and trying to make a living.

Why did we stop making these homes? Buildings that can stand empty for over 100 years and be brought back into a useful condition. Homes made out of what was around them, and with such craftsmanship.

'Because of the cult of convenience,' Brian said to me.

And now we live with that expectation. Like our food that comes to us processed and packaged, and grown with innumerable chemicals, so are many of our houses constructed for us out of treated pine and served up with glues and toxins, at a minimal standard of energy efficiency. We have to use electrical energy, if we can afford it, to heat them.

It doesn't need to be this way. Seven years ago, in a paper put out by the International Energy Agency, an autonomous body of 27 countries, of which New Zealand is a member, it was proposed that energy efficiency in building is such an important issue for countries that government policies must regulate building codes. We must produce houses that are much more efficient than the minimum codes now applying.

'Globally, buildings account for close to 40% of total end use of energy,' the paper says. 'Given the many possibilities to substantially reduce buildings' energy requirements, the potential savings of energy efficiency in the building sector would greatly contribute to a society-wide reduction of energy consumption. The implications of such potential reduction should not be underestimated, as the scale of energy efficiency in buildings is large enough to influence security policy, climate preservation and public health on a national and global scale.'

Though some architects are designing energy-efficient houses with Homestar ratings of 8 and 9 (such as Christchurch architectural designer Bob Burnett), way above the 3-star rating the building code achieves, and there *is* a growing interest in houses that provide all their own energy needs, so much more could be done by regulation to make energy-efficient houses the norm. 'Passive houses

Distinctive stone work and handmade hinges on repaired stable at Highfield.

and zero-energy buildings should be the target for future buildings' codes. A path should be set up to reach this target no later than 2030,' the paper directs.

For now, our building regulation's minimum code has much to do with the fact we build poorly performing homes in this country and pay huge prices for them. The longevity, the heat retention in winter and summer coolness of the original buildings of clay and stone in this area have much to show us for future house design.

And what of the craft of the stonemasons? That rich heritage of craftsmen and tradesmen who came out to New Zealand in the days of the gold rushes. Where each stonemason lived, there are buildings that remain, with their signature style. The stone buildings at Highfield have a distinctive pattern of large square blocks of stone alternating with narrow schist rocks in an undulating pattern; a work of art. Chris Cox said he's seen the same design on the stone buildings in the gold-mining area of Macraes, and we wondered if it had been the same craftsman who built them.

Those stone buildings at Highfield were placed serenely in a large expanse of close-grazed green, with the panorama of mountains in front of them and a grove of black poplars close by. No other buildings or roads or vehicles in sight, just the landscape, and silence. When I drove home I was intensely aware of the road in front of my house, of the cafe, of the cars and trucks and motorbikes. Here was this life dependent on travel and fuel and goods, and there was that other life, in the lee of a hill. The world of the ancestors is still there; the quietness, the crafts-manship, the slower pace. The cottage hunkered down by the rocks, a stream in front for water.

The way we do things now is not the only or the best way of doing things. We are not the only reality.

CHAPTER 25
The Lighthouse Keeper

The high east wall seemed like the last frontier I had to conquer. I set the concrete mixer tumbling with lime and sand. In the garden, the poppies were making a comeback. This morning blue sky, the sun cresting Rough Ridge, the poppies shining with light again.

I stood with my wheelbarrow of plaster and looked up at the high scaffold. When I was plastering mud inside last autumn, standing on top of the ladder with a bucket of mud, I'd been nervous about my broken ribs. When I'd told Brian, he'd said, 'You could have tied a rope to the beam and put it around your waist.'

Good idea. I retrieved a rope from the car, took it inside up to the mezzanine floor, tied it to the main beam and flung the rope out the top window. That's what I'd use for buckets, and for keeping safe.

I filled my blue and green plastic buckets with plaster, tied the rope on one, and climbed the first ladder up the scaffold. When I placed my foot on the second ladder, it felt secure. I looked down. Graeme had screwed small bits of wood around the feet of the ladder to make it safe for me. My scaffold angel!

Up the top, I hauled on the rope till the green bucket came up to the planks. I dropped the rope down again, climbed down, tied the blue bucket on, climbed up and pulled it up to the top. What next? Music, my hawk and trowel, and a hose to wet the wall. (The surface needs to be damp for the new plaster to go on, otherwise the dry first coat sucks too much moisture out of the plaster before it can set.)

I climbed up and down the ladders, hooked up the hose and turned it on, set the music speaker in the doorway and put it on random songs, took my wooden float and hawk over to the foot of the ladder. This was it. I was going to begin plastering the east wall.

As I began to climb the ladder, a song from Curtis Mayfield came on: '... Move

All ready to start plastering the east wall.

on up and keep on wishing. Remember your dream is your only scheme so keep on pushing ...' I smiled to myself at the encouragement.

Five metres above the ground, with the rope tied firmly around my waist, I applied the first trowel load of golden creamy plaster to the apex of the wall. Remembering my dreams and pushing on.

At every moment I was conscious of where my feet were. The fall had taught me the consequences of not staying aware. I'm not renowned for good spatial awareness or even of staying focussed and not dreaming. I think of characters or dialogue while I do something else, running sentences over in my mind. Chris said he doesn't even take his phone up the scaffold in case a call momentarily causes him to lose concentration. I didn't quite go that far, yet I kept my mind clear, absorbed in the stroke-by-stroke meditation of plastering. My arm and the placement of my two feet, that's all I thought about up there.

I smoothed the plaster around the small paned window and out to the eaves. When the buckets were done I threw them off the top, undid my rope, tossed it down and climbed down for more bucket loads. When the wheelbarrow of mix ran out, I made another mix. This was a one-person show now, and nothing to fear. As always it came down to time and intent. A bucket at a time, that's how a wall is done.

All week I'd been waiting for news of a grandchild. That night my son Nick texted from Waiheke Island: *It's started*. Nick and Bex were on an island and Cyclone Pam was heading to New Zealand. At 2 a.m. he texted again. They'd taken the midnight ferry and were now safe at the birthing centre in Auckland.

During the night I woke often, and when the sun rose, Mt Ida diffused with pink light, a soft outline of mountain in a blue sky, there was still no word from Nick.

When daughter Hana had had her first baby, 25 hours crawled past since she'd rung to say contractions were five minutes apart. There was dawn on that day of waiting too, and the tui calling.

I went out to make my first mix of the day. There was a crunch of light frost on the grass and a keen wind coming off the Hawkduns. By mid-morning I was finished on the top scaffold and down to the second tier of planks. After the small apex of the roof, this section of the wall seemed an endless span of mud to cover. How many hours of labour for Bex now? I calculated 15.

Labour is the one time we are at the veil, where birth and death are so closely linked, and the child that is arriving perhaps closest than any of us to what those realms are. 'The not-yet-born, who still know everything,' as poet Mary Oliver writes. For where does a new life truly come from? And why do they sometimes not make it?

I stopped plastering and laid my head against the wall. I cried into the mud surface, giving in to the confusion of emotions of fear and anticipation. One day, I told myself, I'll be able to say to a child, *While you were being born, I made this wall, the one the sun shines on first every morning.* I picked up my trowel, loaded three handfuls of plaster on the hawk and kept going.

On strawbale-raising day, Bridget Henry had turned up from the next valley while her daughter, far away up north, was in labour. Bridget, too, had worked on these walls, waiting for new life.

Twice the phone rang and I fumbled out of my gloves. It was other people. Texts came from my daughters.

Any news?

No, no news.

At 5 p.m. the phone rang again. I was off the scaffold, hosing the back wall to slow down the lime hardening, the very wall Nick and Bex had helped plaster with mud. I pulled the phone out. The caller's name: Nick Sullivan.

'Hello! Hello!' I said. There was a moment's silence. And then the unmistakable cry of a newborn.

Estella.

Once around the whole house. Nine days' work. A celebratory coffee in the old mudbrick cafe in Hayes Engineering. I wanted to see the plasterer Ross, tell him *I've done it!* But he wasn't there. He was off sourcing cow shit for a mud mix to plaster inside walls. I wanted to come back the next day and watch him make and apply the plaster, but I had my own walls to do. The project of plastering the house all over again.

About an hour into the second coat, up on the top scaffold, I put down my float with frustration. I'd plastered the house with one small wooden float and now I couldn't bear it any longer. It was small and light to use, but edging around each joist at the junction of the roof and wall was so difficult. Plaster fell off over and over again. How did you get around edges? I gave up, climbed down and rang my Uncle Ken, 86, and blind now, and still a fount of stories of Dad and him and their life as plasterers.

'You used a wooden float for the whole job?' he asked.

'Yes, because the steel trowel kept chopping into the plaster.'

On the top scaffold, west wall.

'But the steel trowel is designed for getting the plaster off your hawk and up the wall. You did the whole house yourself? Made all the plaster?'

'Sam helped on the first wall. And Graeme. Then I did everything else,' I said. 'I had to keep getting down from the scaffold to get the concrete mixer going.'

'You did a great job then. I did a house by myself once, in the 1960s. It was out at Castlepoint. I had everything organised, the sand delivered, the scaffolds up. But I couldn't get our big concrete mixer off the trailer by myself. Now what was I going to do? I looked up the road, and there was the Lighthouse Keeper walking along. He came and helped me lift it off. I paid him a few bob to come and run the concrete mixer for me. That's what you need, someone like a Lighthouse Keeper.'

Before I climbed back up the scaffold, I sorted through a box in the carport and found the old steel trowel. I looked for a triangular pointy trowel, a gauging trowel, but I didn't have one in the collection of tools Sam and I had picked up from recycle shops.

'A gauging trowel, that's the most important tool you can have,' Uncle Ken had said. 'That will get you round all the tricky corners. I'd go up on the scaffold with a bucket of water for cleaning my tools, my trowels, float and hawk, a small tool for scraping and a 3-foot rule.'

'I wish I'd rung you before I started, Uncle Ken,' I said.

'And if I wasn't blind and so stiff, I'd come down and help you,' he said.

I started again on the top planks, this time with the steel trowel to cut the plaster and smooth it up the wall. How much easier it seemed. My arm was stronger now after nine days plastering. I had more control of the plaster. The work went much faster. Why didn't I get the right tools when I first started?

I said that to Graeme, when he called round later to see how I was getting on. 'I've done it all the hard way before I learnt,' I said.

'Everything I learnt building I learnt by doing the wrong thing first,' he said.

'You know what you are? You're a Lighthouse Keeper,' I said. 'The way you fixed the ladder for me so it was safe, and how you always encourage me.' I told him Uncle Ken's story.

'Everyone needs a Lighthouse Keeper,' said Graeme.

Plastering took over my life. That was the only way I could get it done – to stay deep in the process until it was over. Sometimes I didn't know how I'd do everything that needed to be done: water the new tussocks, edit a friend's writing, finish a community job I offered to do, work at the hospital, hose the new plaster, eat. When would I write and face the novel again, and would I be able to write another decent poem? And what about my mother, when would I see her again, or my children?

Sometimes the process of building is messy, complex, painful, lonely. And yet to be able to do it – what a privilege.

CHAPTER 26

Raw Milk and a Donkey's Breakfast

Once more I was running late, on a road I'd never been on before and I'd left the directions behind on the bench. Somewhere up ahead in the fog was the dairy farm and raw milk for my experimental lime wash. The lime-plastered walls had dried out for ten days, and it was time to begin applying the finish coats. Was this still Ranfurly-Patearoa Rodd? Each turn I took driving meant a decision that could take me further from the right direction.

I experience that same nervous propulsion sometimes when writing – once I commit to cause and effect, my character can be a long way down a trail I hadn't expected to explore. Yet I'd learnt to trust that impulse in writing – the trail I'm on is the one I'm supposed to be on – so I kept driving.

There were no cows in sight, a gravel road I could see for only 20 metres ahead of me, and a billowing mist across the paddocks. There was a number on a gate, and I remembered this was the one and turned up a driveway. Kate Herlihy came to the door of an old villa, a small blonde daughter shy behind her. Kate pulled her gumboots on and we went out to the drive.

'I went up to the shed this morning for the milk,' she said, and lifted a large bucket out of her truck.

'Can I help you with that?'

'No, it's fine.' She placed it on the floor behind my front seat.

'How much do I owe you?'

'Nothing,' she said. 'It's our contribution to the house.'

It wasn't until I lifted the bucket of milk out of my car I realised how heavy it was. Twenty litres of raw milk, with a smell as clear as water.

There was no fog back in the Ida, instead damp soil and a grey sky, the plants upright in the garden and the air calm. Not the raw wind and rain that late yesterday had hammered the trees and flowers. Only the tussocks had shrugged about it. Now they lolled, rain beaded. A few new poppies had water in their cups.

Barry's steers, brown with white faces, were clumped by the fence in my paddock, waiting for something.

'You know, humans could learn a lot from animals,' Barry had said to me once. 'It's amazing the things you see and learn from watching them.' He told me of a ewe who had triplets one year. Barry's wife, Joy, called out to him one day, 'Come and look at this, it's not triplets, it's actually a single and twins.' They watched the mother, and heard how she first gave one sort of bleat and the single came running for a feed, and then she nudged it away. She called out with a different bleat and the twins came running up to her for their feed.

'Those lambs all grew at the same rate, too,' Barry said.

And I liked his bull story.

'A neighbour brought over 200 cows and five bulls to one of my paddocks,' Barry told us one night at a dinner at Graeme and Donna's. 'There was an old bull amongst them, and first thing, those four younger bulls gave him a thrashing. The old bull went and lay down under a tree and those four other bloody bulls just kept scrapping. Meanwhile there's cows coming on heat every day. Six or seven at a time. They lined up under the tree waiting their turn with the old bull. Those young bulls wouldn't stop fighting and they missed out.'

I considered the milk in the bucket at my feet. The lime-wash recipe from the plasterer down south, via Chris Cox who used it on his stone stables, is one-part slaked lime, one-part raw skim milk and two-parts water.

Another plasterer, also experienced on historic houses, had told me he wouldn't use milk in lime washes. He'd seen it grow mould on a house. His recipe is one-part lime to three-parts water. Two opposite opinions. When I was trying to make up my mind about which recipe to use, I'd rung my uncle again.

'We used to make lime wash with mutton fat, salt, water and lime,' Uncle Ken had said. 'Then for a house we worked on for Riddifords, the architect specified skim milk for the lime wash. Riddifords had a farm, so George and I took the truck up to the shed with a 44-gallon drum on it and they filled it with milk. That lime wash was beautiful.'

Milk adds casein to lime wash, for added weather protection. It doesn't affect the permeability of the lime wash, and that's the most important factor. The lime wash needs to let the house breathe so any dampness in the straw can come out. The old recipe of using mutton fat is called a tallow lime wash. The fat helps with weather tightness, but it affects permeability, so for natural houses it is not suitable.

Kate said the milk would last for about four days. I carried the heavy bucket inside, put most of the milk in containers in the fridge and took a small bucket out to the back of the house. I had my white overalls on. They were an essential requirement, not just for protection from the caustic lime, but also to help me feel professional when I was facing a job I didn't know how to do. It's like when I go cycling, especially for a tough ride with Brian. I put on my cycle shorts and top and pull on the black wrist gloves, and I mean business.

I haven't worked out a uniform for writing yet.

Under the back verandah I considered my mixing options. I chose a black plastic rubbish bin as my mixer, put two ice-cream containers of the slaked lime into it, two containers of the fresh skimmed milk and four containers of water. How much yellow oxide to tint it? For making the lime plaster I'd tinted it at around one heaped soup spoon of oxide to a 10-litre bucket of plaster. I put in one and a half spoonfuls of the yellow powder and whisked the mixture. It turned into a deep buttery colour, the thickness of runny cream. I picked up my brush. Now to see how it worked.

I began with the back wall, the one most exposed to weather and also out of sight of the road for colour experiments.

'Hose the wall first,' Uncle Ken had told me. And take a brushful and spread it out, then follow the lime down as it runs. It should run down the wall. Work it in.'

'What sort of brush should I use?' I'd asked.

'We used one we called a donkey's breakfast,' Ken said. 'Big 8-ounce grass brush. It holds lots of lime. And it looks like something a donkey could eat.'

I did try asking at the plaster shop in Queenstown if they had a donkey's breakfast, but it seemed to be a term limited to use by G. Masters & Sons Ltd, Masterton. The next time I went back in, though, they had brought in some hair brushes that looked a little edible, and proved to do a good job.

I had imagined the lime wash would go on like paint, a thick covering. But with five coats as a minimum, I guess the first coat was always going to be a subtle one, and it was. It didn't cover all my imperfections and smooth them out. It hardly made a difference. There was still the unevenly ridged plaster under the first coat of lime wash.

This was the most difficult wall we'd put straw in and mud on. The wall had bulges where it shouldn't. I learnt that the straighter you make the wall right from the start, when the straw bales go in, the easier every application is after that. It was the first wall Sam and I had plastered and Graeme and I had covered over. There was a lot of learning going on with this wall! One coat of thinned-down lime wasn't in a hurry to fix it. It is the back wall, though, and each night in the setting sun with the Hawkduns behind it, the house's imperfections melt into the wider view.

The tarpaulins were gone from the east side of the house. This was the wall exposed to the road and the easterly rain. Two coats of dry lime plaster protected the mud walls now, and in preparation for the final work on the house – five coats of lime wash – I'd pulled the tarpaulins down. No longer hidden inside the grey-sheeted world of the scaffolds, I had a good view of the goings-on in the valley. Though the air had a piquancy of chill in it, a warning of winter to come, the farmers were planning for spring. Down the road came the matrons of the valley, the sturdy-shouldered Romney-Merino ewes, going to the shed in the paddock behind the village for pre-tup crutching, and then they'd be off to the rams.

The wall beside the new red front door was the area Sven Johnston had mud-plastered when he was teaching us. The bales were stacked straight and Sven's mud plaster was even. The straighter walls had made my lime plastering look skilful, and the lime wash here was everything I'd hoped for. Pearly, radiant. The house soon started to look and feel like an old fishing cottage on the coast of Wales.

Environmentally, the best reason for using lime is that it fixes carbon from the atmosphere. Any carbon that is used to make the lime is collected again into the walls. When limestone is crushed and burnt in limestone kilns, the intense heat (up to 1000°C) drives off water and carbon dioxide from the lime. The lime changes from calcium carbonate to calcium oxide. Calcium oxide is the product known as quicklime, or burnt lime.

When you slake burnt lime, adding it back to water, a huge amount of heat is generated (as my rocking drums testified), hydrogen is taken on by the calcium oxide, and calcium hydroxide is formed. This is the lime putty, the creamy-white mix you store in drums.

Lime putty is then mixed with sand and applied to the wall as plaster. Here's the best part. The lime begins to react with carbon dioxide, incorporating it, and returns to calcium carbonate; in other words, it returns to its original form of limestone on the wall. A carbon-neutral process.

From a building perspective, the best things about lime are its intensely alkaline nature that keeps it hygienic, prohibiting mould and mildew; its ability to heal its own cracks during the many years' process of carbonation; its easy workability, and lime is vapour permeable. An exterior render of lime plaster allows any moisture in a house to dry out.

In comparison, Portland cement was invented in 1842 and began to be used extensively in concrete preparation from 1850. After World War II, cement stucco replaced lime plastering on houses all over the United Kingdom and Europe. People embraced the new medium. No more two-to-ten yearly maintenance schedules of lime washing. Put it up once and forget it. But what the one-time application and unmaintained render of cement did on the houses was cover up the problems inside. Damp lingers. Cement is not permeable like lime. Behind their facades, the houses of traditional materials began to deteriorate. In cob, stone, mud and timber walls, mould and damp and rot flourished.

'It happened to our house in Wales too,' Leslie Davies told me. 'We had to chip off the cement plaster and put lime back on.'

All over Wales, she told me, people replaced the cement with lime on their old houses to save them. Skills with lime had to be re-learnt. A skill that had been useful for thousands of years had begun to die out with the invention of cement.

Leslie told me that one woman who, as a novice, took on plastering her stone cottage with lime, has since gone on to be such a respected plasterer, she had the job of restoring lime render on the houses of royalty. I liked this story very much!

Putting on limewash suited my happy, slap-dash nature. I could mix a batch of 8 litres in a matter of minutes and be up on the scaffold, music on, singing along. At last, after the long haul of the house, an easy job. Slurp, slush, on with the lime. A heavy brushful, follow it down as it runs on the wall. Easy. No thick, quick-drying paint to negotiate or be finicky about. Lime washing is a joyous job.

It still needs protective clothing, however. After I'd reached above my head with a full brush-load and accidentally splashed lime in behind my sunglasses, I had to spend an uncomfortable 30 minutes in the shower flushing my eye out and dousing it with watered-down vinegar.

The process of successive coats, building up millimetre by millimetre over the imperfections, over the swirls of plastering, over tiny cracks, over changes in colour or texture, is perhaps a metaphor for life as well. In time, with consistent effort and repeated brush strokes, faults can be erased.

Lime-washing was like putting makeup on the house. There – a flawless cheek to the world. Well, never *flawless*. The house still invites a hand to come and follow its slight curves and dips. And I want to touch it. I press my nose to it, like I would to Gypsy's neck, inhaling the tomato-leaf sweet tang of her. My house smells of milk, like melted ice cream, and is the colour of French Vanilla.

'Mmmm, listen to the sound of the house breathing,' Chris said when he called in for the scaffolding. Lime-wash spattered scaffolding now.

'That doesn't matter,' he said. 'It's going to get a whole lot worse in September. Will you come and help plaster my house?' he asked.

'Yes!'

'It will be time for a party,' he said.

The stone stables he's rebuilding and turning into a house has one long, high-walled room at the back, 70 square metres of it; four stone walls. The ballroom, Chris calls it. It used to be the granary, the wooden-floored room where grain was stored. He knows of five other granaries in the district. Because of their size and the sprung floors, they were often used by the community for holding dances. You can still see on the wall in Chris's room the card suits of heart, club, spade and diamond for organising the dance.

Now Chris was assembling a team to take on the plastering of these stone walls. I'd be back on the mixer. I'd be up on the scaffolding with my hawk and trowel and the new gauging trowel I bought after I'd finished plastering my house.

There's something about a naturally built house that invites a team. It's the forgiving nature of the materials – especially mud. It's the tactile experience of hands on, and hands in.

My brother Scott, who worked plastering with Dad for eight years, came with his wife Nicole and their three children one weekend and plastered an interior bedroom wall with me. It was Scott's first contact with a natural mud plaster. He found it went on smoothly, and unlike gypsum plaster, it didn't go off in the bucket (set) but remained pliable and usable for hours. *Days*, I told him. He tried out different techniques, trowelling and re-trowelling the mud. He even gave eight-year-old Finn the trowel and let him have a go.

There's no hassle with mud, no rush to get it perfect before it goes hard. And when we required more mud, the whole family went out to make it. Aimee, Finn and Benji needed no encouragement to get into the bath of mud and trample it with their feet, helping combine the different mixer loads in the bath.

When it came time to lime wash the interior bedroom walls, a new friend and neighbour, Angela McKnight, came to help me.

'I don't mind heights,' she said, and joined me on the plank. I'd taped plastic sheets over the windows to protect the glass and timber joinery, which meant there was no fresh air in the room. The first coat was hard work: first, wetting the dry mud-walls by brush (no easy hosing inside), and second, applying lime wash to a sucky mud medium. Talking and laughing helped. That first coat took four hours, and worse than that, there was an intense, almost overpowering smell of wet mud in the enclosed room. (I learnt to do this stage with windows open for the rest of the house.)

The next layer, lime on top of lime, took only a quarter of the time, with no smell. A much faster, smoother and more enjoyable application. All up, I did six coats of lime wash on the walls, with 24-hours' drying time between them to allow for the fixing of carbon dioxide into the lime.

As for lime wash dripping on the floor, I didn't worry about it. I gave the concrete floor six coats of lime wash as well, after the walls were done. Has anyone done that before? I couldn't find any information on it, not even from plastering shops. I like the finish. The floors have the same soft, pearly radiance as the walls. It's not a hardened finish, furniture scrapes it, though I can easily and for little cost put another coat on some day. Until carpet comes, the lime-washed floors, to me, are a thing of beauty in the house.

Last summer, six rural women from the Kakanui Mountains district drove over to see my house after they'd heard me being interviewed about it on National Radio. They brought their overalls and gumboots. They made mud with me, a beautiful, silky mix we could use straight after lunch for them to have a go at plastering. We plastered the last half of the front wall of the house, making it, finally, safe from wandering cows. The women sang *Michael row your boat ashore, Hallelujah!* (two of them were in a choir), and laughed, and gave me sound advice:

'Put a good-sized stone with water in your concrete mixer to clean it.'

'Wipe fresh mortar with a wet cloth,' (after inspecting the stone fireplace).

And the third piece of advice I scribbled in my notebook: 'Plump your boobs together to make them look firmer.'

How that one came about in between wheelbarrow, mud and concrete mixer, I'm not sure. But when the women left, the wall was done, we'd shared a meal, and aspects of our lives.

It is possible to plaster a house alone. I'd proved that to myself. And lime wash it. But it's good to share the task with others, too, and laugh, and in between, weave our stories.

185

CHAPTER 27

The Tenaciousness of Rocks

'Are you two free this afternoon?' Robert Gardyne asked Brian and I at the Ida Valley Kitchen cafe one day in February 2015. 'I've got something special to show you up on the farm. I'll take you up on the motorbike.'

I'd first got to know Robert at the Brass Monkey Rally. After a weekend of cutting pumpkins, cooking and serving food for the rally, and the big Sunday clean-up, it's a tradition for the helpers to gather in the pub for a shared lunch, put on by the pub owners.

Robert and his family were newcomers like me. We'd stood in the crowd at the pub, amongst people who would be our new community. Robert told me of the day he and Rosemary and their family had finally left their old farm. It took 18 truckloads to shift all their stock and machinery from the farm down south to a new life here in the Maniototo.

'The evening I drove down our road with the last load, I cried,' he said. 'It's hard to leave behind the land you love and start again.'

'I did the same,' I said. 'I lived near Motueka for 30 years before I came down here. That's a long time to have friends and leave them.'

'It's the most difficult part of all,' he said. 'We had to leave behind folk whose weddings we'd been to, their bereavements, the births of their children, all the sports days, pet days, cross-country days, school concerts and community events. The tapestry of their lives had become a big part of the tapestry of our lives. The most difficult part of shifting is the people you have to wrench yourself away from.'

Brian and I met Robert outside his farmhouse, suitably dressed in jackets and hats though it was summer. We jumped on the back of Robert's quad bike, and he accelerated up the farm track, heading for the tops, 3000 feet above sea level.

All the years on our own block of land, also 3000-feet high, when Dave had driven the motorbike, I'd sat on the back, in hat and gloves and jacket, our food supplies in a box on the front and our daughter Evie wedged between us, warm and safe. Sometimes her cat Marmite came with us, zipped into the front of Dave's jacket.

For once I felt no melancholy at this memory – just an acknowledgement of what has passed; that I had had that life and a partner and small children, and rocks and matagouri and bracken on the way to beech trees hundreds of years old.

Later, I considered why I hadn't been struck by sadness and loss from the memories the farm trip evoked. For the land up the mountain and our hut is sold now. There can be no returning, no walking up that last slope to the weathered door, or the final grunt of the motorbike up the track and the sky opening up to forest and a hut on the edge of a clearing.

Not even in hope can I go back now, for Evie has grown; she's six inches taller than me, has a degree in biomedical science and lives in the city. Those days are like the days of childhood – a territory imprinted in you that can never be re-lived. Our childhood lives are what make us, and who we are now belongs to that time; we cannot pass back to it. We can only live each moment from then on, making new and coherent histories.

A child growing up and leaving home is a rightness of loss. It is lost love we are haunted by: opportunities to be kind we didn't take, and times we didn't choose patience, or to not be right, or to listen. To be willing to stand stripped of dignity – by the illusions we hold of ourselves as someone righteous, someone who knows best, to be unclothed of our own moral remembering and be unprotected, and in this way to listen to another's pain. That is the challenge I failed at so often.

There is no inevitability of growth, like there is of girl to woman or boy to man. There is just this stumbling forward as an adult, this 'perilous and fearful effort' as Wendell Berry puts it, that we make at relationships, which must 'endure the blundering of ignorance'.

This is where partnerships can be renewed, repaired, or broken – by our own responses: not by the outside effects of financial struggle or conjoined families or the differing expectations one has of the other, but of the way one chooses to be.

On Robert's motorbike in the bright sun, with the far jagged-rock horizon ahead of us up an adventurous track, I recalled my times of jouncing up the farm track as a family squeezed together, with the rightness of something that has passed.

Yet here in the Ida Valley there is again, unexpectedly, tussock and rock and wild brambles, a good friend on the front of the bike and Brian beside me on the back, his notebook in my pocket.

We parked on the slope and walked down through silver tussock and billowy snow grass, round the side of the cliff where Robert stopped.

'There,' he said.

At first I didn't know what he meant, I was too busy concentrating on the track to see what was in front of us. In that landscape of ice-cracked rock, snowy winds and parching summers, a tree grew, almost out of rock. An ancient kowhai tree. Its trunk twisted and curved above us, and out of reach there were green fronds, and also dead branches and twigs. Dieback from the drought.

'Kowhais don't grow in the Maniototo,' Robert said. 'Yet this one is hundreds of years old. It's taken a hammering this year. But it's thriving. How, I don't know. When I think of what it's gone through to make it, through all those hard winters.' He looked around at the steep valley slopes. 'It gets all the wind here, but the morning sun, too.

'My son and I saw the silhouette of this tree from down on the flats one day, but it took us two years to find it. I have a lot of respect for this tree.'

It seems to me this is the best we can hope for, for land – to have someone who owns it who knows the land, who can see what needs doing and does it, whose animals are well cared for, and who has a reverence for the features of the land, the trees, the rocks, the springs – for the gifts that they are – and protects them. A consideration for all living things. And whose concerns are wider than the farm, and embraces the community as well.

We climbed back up to the bike and Robert drove us through golden tus-socked hills higher and higher into the land of rocky tors; Hobbit land. Peter Jackson had filmed some of *The Lord of the Rings* trilogy and *The Hobbit* up here amongst the rocks and far horizons. There's a rock like a triangular mountain on top of the hill where the Hobbits enter, in the film, and come out into landscape in the Mackenzie country.

I'd been on the set of *The Fellowship of the Ring* one day as a guest. My son Rory was a Gondorian soldier, and daughter Hana the minder for Viggo Mortensen, who played Aragorn in the film. I'd sat at lunch with Hobbits, dwarves, and sol-diers with gaping wounds.

Here, I walked up to the Hobbit rock, a triangle maybe 20 metres high with a dark cleft, like an entrance to a cave. I placed my hands on the bronzy, ridged rock. The cave on the film set that day with Hana was made from polystyrene and painted charcoal grey. Fires burned around me in small pyres, and sackclothed adults and children waited in dark corners. It felt so real I could have morphed into the pages of the book. From the darkness of the cave, just a few metres in front of me, I watched the leader of the dwarves and Aragorn in a scene.

'Cut. That was great,' Peter Jackson said. 'How about one more time?'

'All quiet on set. Rolling,' a voice called. I stood watching, absorbed in the scene. Then I felt an urge to cough. I swallowed, and swallowed. Around me everyone was silent. My throat burned. Oh no, a solid piece of acting about to be ruined by someone's mother lurking in the shadows. I backed out of the cave and ran wildly downhill until I was far enough away, then doubled over and coughed and coughed.

On the farm this day there was silence. The rocks towered over us. Rocks that had been pushed out of the earth on an earthquake fault, born out of tussocked land; slabs of rock, tilted, perched, and sometimes slabs on top of slabs, most pointing in the same direction – northeast. And each rock colonised in cracks by tussock, matagouri, Spaniard grass. The rocks held a presence up on that ridge that spoke of mighty forces, of rupturing, and cataclysmic thrusting, of endurance. No wonder this place was chosen for films of heroic journeys. In amongst the rocks I felt small, soft, short-lived.

When we came back down from the top I had fragments of rock and bone in my pocket and a goat's shoulder bone in my hand. A white bone so light I thought that must be a good way to return to the earth: imperceptibly.

From the car on the way home, the hills became a horizon again, the tors just those rocks on the skyline. Yet the memory of being amongst them, of once again being out in the aloneness of hill and rock and sky, was inside me. Something of tenaciousness to recall and to try and live by.

At home, Mt Ida had gone grey, and the last of the sun lit up the western flanks of the Hawkduns. In the front paddock, Barry's heifers meandered and chewed, soothed by 20 acres of good grass, my ungrazed paddocks a boon for them in the drought.

Last year the grasses in the paddock were so long they turned silver in the setting sun. The cocksfoot and timothy waved like tussock and the light rippled across their grains. Now the grass is nibbled down and the brown beasts mooch fatly by. There are no flocks of birds rising out of the seeded heads of grasses, yet on my banks the wild flowers thrive and so do bees.

CHAPTER 28

Hello House

After months of drought during the summer of 2015, the Ida Burn had emptied all the way towards Wedderburn. When Indy and Phoenix came to stay, they ran and clambered over dry river stones the length of my property, except for where water lay in a remnant of our swimming hole. In that darkened, sluggish water, Phoenix saw a long, lean trout. We rescued it in a well-executed mission with local Fish & Game officer Trevor Beck, his son Andrew, and Brian. The trout and 50 koura were restored to Trevor's bigger, wider pond up the road.

My own pond had dried up in the drought, as had the five potable springs in the front paddock that fed it. Barry said he hadn't seen those springs dry up in 50 years. There's been more intensification of agriculture on the land in the valley, and no rain, no rain, and the farms all around with their tawny, dusty slopes.

Then, in autumn, a one-in-fifty-year flood hit further up the coast and brought torrents of rain to this side of the Kakanui and Ida ranges.

I looked up from my desk and saw with surprise the pond was full again. I left my laptop, pulled on gumboots and a jacket and went across the paddock. Two paradise ducks, in a flash of black and brown and white, flew up from the rushes on the banks of the pond. My first parries. Last year there were little grey ducks, and fifteen ducklings that gradually dwindled to none, and then they were gone.

The pond, in the shelter of willows, was full to the brim; a sheen of blue sky and white cloud between grassy banks. I stood near the small stream issuing from the pond, a clattery, ripply flow of water heading once more across the paddock.

Beyond the willows, a shushing of river noise. I picked my way over recently flooded pasture and came to the Ida Burn. It was a turbulent, rushing body of water. The young willows on the opposite side were speckled with cheeping sparrows. I walked beside the muddy water, remembering places that now held new memories – the place under the old willow where we found the trout, the first swimming hole until the stream changed course, the picnic spot I shared with

Indy, the bank where I'd picked up flat stones for the ensuite floor. Everything covered over, and further up, the bank mangled and taken by water. There the Ida Burn raged, 7 metres wide. I could see one day, after more of these same floods, the stream could change course again, maybe take out some of my lower paddock. For such is the response of water, the whim and strength of it.

When I was considering laying small river stones for the ensuite floor, son Nick had said to me, 'People who have money and not much time pay others to work on their houses, and people who don't have much money, and have time, can work on their own houses. That's you, Mum. You should do the stones.'

But not *that* much spare time, I thought, in the middle of grouting the stones. A laborious 40 hours of spooning and smoothing grout around uneven pebbles.

American author Michael Pollan, in his book *A Place of My Own*, described sanding timber for his house as 'exquisite drudgery' and I understood what he meant. Hours and hours of the same repeated actions and the unrelenting concentration, but the bright promise of a finished and beautiful work.

Nick helped me start laying the stones, and Nelson writer and friend Jessica Le Bas came and helped me carry on. We shared a common amazement when stones began to fit together in a flow.

Finding the small flat stones became one of the most enjoyable processes of building the house. Often a walk beside a river means just that, the eye roving over water and stones and sky and light. Choosing stones means the eye travels from one stone to the next, stone after stone after stone, immersed in their detail, while the rushy water clinkers in the background to the smell of hot sand and minerals. Much of the enjoyment comes from the simplicity of being right in that moment, and what better moment to be in than next to a clear and burbling stream.

One late afternoon, Brian called in to see how it was going. I'd run out of stones and had the last of a bucket of freshly made grout. We strode over the paddocks in the sunset to the stream, and in the fading light bent over and picked and discarded and sorted, till there were enough for half a bucket each of stones to finish the final portion of floor.

The day before, I'd been down collecting stones in the sun. I'd straightened up and stood for a few moments watching the water enter and swirl into a deep jade pond. Something plunged into the water in front of me, a small object, catapulted from the sky.

I stared at the water. It was a baby rabbit. It swam in hesitant circles. My mind

couldn't assimilate it for a moment. I looked around, and up at the sky. Nothing. But the rabbit was true. It was right in front of my eyes.

I watched the rabbit to be sure it was safe. It found the edge of the bank and clambered up, and sat there, hunched over small, recovering. When I told my mother about it later, I asked her, *What would you take from this story*? For surely, the baby rabbit had been dropped by a flying hawk. First, it was on its way to be eaten. Then it was dropped, most likely to its death. But it landed in a small space of water and was saved.

'That however difficult life seems,' my mother said, 'you don't know what unexpected event is about to come along and save you.'

Or change you.

The house is nearly done. The lime plaster and lime wash are all finished, so that in last week's torrential rain the house stood safe in its protective cloak, the lime wash turning butter-yellow again on the walls while they were wet.

I walked back from the Ida Burn across the paddocks and stopped at the woodpile to chop a few rounds of willow into smaller logs. It is almost winter again. The Hawkduns certainly know so. They are white-flanked, the late sun smouldering shadows in the gullies. Now that the willows by the pond have lost their leaves, I can see Mt St Bathans too, way across the valley.

My mother taught me, in her bereavement, we don't want loss, we don't want this dark upheaval in our life, but sometimes that's what we get, a brand new start, and we have to do what we can and make a life worth living from there.

How? I thought about that as wood split open. By honouring who you are, for a start. And the family you come from, the people beside you, the community you live in, and the land that holds you.

The wind was getting up again, a nor'wester. The tussocks bent to it and the toetoe. The few broom bushes in the paddock stood stiffly and shook. The feel of snow was in the air.

Yesterday, when a gale was forecast, Brian and I had ridden out early, hoping to beat the wind. It caught us out at the top of Ida Valley. As we swung into the wind up Lockhart's Hill, on the way to St Bathans, cycling became an exercise in how to keep upright and pedalling, and how, in gusts, to stay on the bike at all. Though Brian wasn't so perturbed. More experienced with bikes and wind, he could look around him, and even lifted his arm to point down the valley: 'Look at that snow on the Old Woman Range.'

Back on the Ida straights, the wind came at us sideways, the cloud low and dense over Blackstone Hill, as if soon there would be more snow.

'It's a hard ride on the road,' Brian said from up ahead, sounding like a cowboy.

I held the door against the wind, willow logs in my other arm, and stepped inside the house to a quietness and shelter. Though the fire wasn't lit, the house held an undisturbed warmth. The quietness and stillness has much to do with the faint smell of straw and sunlight on earth.

'Hello house,' I said, as I always do, coming in.

On the walls are paintings by my Nelson friends, Venetia Hill, Melita Johnston, Linda Hannan – the sea and sky and colour of Tasman Bay, and a new one, Jessica Le Bas's pastel drawing of the strawbale house. On the fridge, photos of my children: Nick holding baby Estella in his arms, Evie aged 12 on her horse Quartz on Mt Pukeone, all five grown-up children, Hana, Merrin, Rory, Nick and Evie, when they surprised me at my book launch. There's a newspaper photo of Brian and me performing at the Maniototo Bards and Ballads, and of my old band, Red Dress. There are paintings from Indy, and from Australian granddaughters Ela, Lacey and Scarlett, titled, 'Grandma I Love You'. There's a photo of my father in white overalls (the month before he died) and he is plastering.

I kneel down with the logs and some pine cones to light the fire. When it's cheery, I set a pot of soup on top. Take up my pen and notebook.

In the house there is still lime plastering to be done in the bathroom, and a bedroom ceiling, more skirting boards and architraves, and lights to be wired in, another coat of mud in the sitting room ...

Lists and lists. But that's all right. I'm here now.

Bibliography

Berry, Wendell, *The Long-Legged House*, Berkeley, 2012

Berry, Wendell, *What Matters: Economics for a Renewed Commonwealth*, Counterpoint Press, 2010

Berry, Wendell, *The Art of the Commonplace: The Agrarian Essays of Wendell Berry*, Shoemaker and Hoard, 2002

Berry, Wendell, *Standing by Words*, Counterpoint Press, 1983

Bethell, Ursula, 'Response' (1929), In Vincent O'Sullivan (ed.), *Collected Poems*, Victoria University Press, 1997

Campbell, Joseph, *The Hero of a Thousand Faces*, Fontana Press, 1993

Estés, Clarissa Pinkola, *Women Who Run With the Wolves: Myths and Stories of the Wild Woman Archetype*, Ballentyne, 1992

Goodrich, Charles, *The Practice of Home: Biography of a House*, The Lyons Press, 2004

Hegel, G.W.F., *The Phenomenology of Spirit* (1807), A.V. Miller trans., Clarendon Press, 1977

Hesse, Hermann, *Siddhartha*, Picador, 1973

Jung, Carl, *Memories, Dreams, Reflections*, Vintage Books, 1965, p. 212

Larkin, Charlotte Preston, *Puawananga: The Adobe Cottage*, Russell Centennial Trust Board, 2004

Leopold, Aldo, *A Sand County Almanac, and Sketches Here and There*, Oxford University Press, 1949

Oliver, Mary, *White Pine: Poems and Prose Poems*, Harcourt, 1994

Pollan, Michael, *A Place of My Own: The Education of an Amateur Builder*, Random House, 1999

Steen, Athena and Bill, *The Beauty of Straw Bale Homes*, Chelsea Green, 2001

Sullivan, Jillian, 'Wind in the Ida', *Meniscus* 2(1): www.meniscus.org.au/volume-2-issue-1-2

Thoreau, Henry David, *Works of Henry David Thoreau* (1906), Crown Publishers, 1981

Turner, Brian, *Just This*, Victoria University Press, 2009

Vitruvius, *The Ten Books on Architecture*, available from Project Gutenberg: http://www.gutenberg.org/files/20239/20239-h/29239-h.htm

Acknowledgements

With grateful thanks to all who supported me and helped create the strawbale house:

Sam and Hana Deavoll, Brian Turner, Graeme and Donna Male, Barry and Joy Becker, Dennis Deavoll, Rory Sullivan, Nick and Bex Sullivan, Evie Haverkort, Merrin and George Robinson, Indy Deavoll, Julie Deavoll, Chris Cox, Quentin McFeat, Bridget Auchmuty, Pat Shuker, Philippa and Barbara Pope, Declan Wong, Anataia and Kiriana Wong, Bridget Henry, Bob L de Berry, Grahame Sydney, Gary Mills, Greg Tump, Sven and Sarah Johnston, Grant Harris, Grim Corfield, Colin Leishman, Tom Moran, Beckers Transport, Trevor and Judy Beck, Paddy Beck, Antonia Cooney, Charly Le Bonté, Andre Lopez-Turner, RJ Roush and Natalie Okun, Bailey Brooks, Angela Wilson, Angela McKnight, Sonia and Mark Dillon, Gordon Scott, Sam Forsyth, Corey Robinson, Bruce Hannan and Melita Johnston, Jessica Le Bas, Zona Averill, Ken Masters, Scott and Nicole Masters, Aimee, Finn and Benji Masters, Steve Aldridge and Paula Wagemaker, Graham Wardrop, Richard Anderson, Graeme McKnight, Heather Gilchrist, Jack and Vivienne McClean, Vicky Wills, Jeannine Bradley, Ross Miller, Kate Herlihy, Isobel Thom, Joy Cowley and Terry Cole, Jasio Zyzwalo and Julie Grieg, and the Central Otago District Council.

Photo Credits

Declan Wong: pp. 7, 9, 25, 49, 71, 113, 149
Michaela Cox: pp. 8, 147, 191, 193
Graham Wardrop: p. 177
Sam Deavoll: pp. 28, 61, 121, 127
Jillian Sullivan: pp. 13, 14, 50, 70, 75, 81, 89, 91, 94, 97, 99, 110, 112, 117, 128, 144, 155, 162, 169, 171, 174

Published in 2016 by Potton & Burton
98 Vickerman Street, PO Box 5128, Nelson, New Zealand
www.pottonandburton.co.nz

© Jillian Sullivan
Cover photography by Grahame Sydney
Cover and internal design: Lisa Noble, Paperminx
Edited by: Judith Watson

ISBN 978 0 947503 26 0

Printed in China by Midas Printing International